What they've said about Nineteenth-century Statesmen

A selection of source material by

FRANK E. HUGGETT

OXFORD UNIVERSITY PRESS 1972

Oxford University Press, Ely House, London W.1

Glasgow	Cape Town	Bombay	Kuala Lumpur
New York	Salisbury	Calcutta	Singapore
Toronto	Ibadan	Madras	Hong Kong
Melbourne	Nairobi	Karachi	Tokyo
Wellington	Dar es Salaam	Lahore	
	Lusaka	Dacca	
	Addis Ababa		

By the same author

What they've said about . . . Nineteenth-century Reformers,
Oxford University Press, 1971
A Short History of Farming, Macmillan, 1970
How it Happened, Basil Blackwell, 1971
Travel and Communications, A Documentary Inquiry,
Harrap, 1972

Photoset by Typesetting Services Ltd., Glasgow and printed in Great Britain at the University Press, Oxford, by Vivian Ridler, Printer to the University.

What they've said about . . .
**Nineteenth-century
Statesmen**

Palmerston

Disraeli

Peel

Salisbury

Gladstone

Contents

Preface

This book of source material presents some nineteenth-century statesmen in many different lights. Extracts from accounts written at the time reveal the contemporary reactions to some of the major controversial issues in which they were involved, including Catholic emancipation, the repeal of the Corn Laws, the Don Pacifico case, Home Rule, and 'splendid isolation'. There are extracts from the statesmen's own speeches and publications, and from those of their supporters and critics. The statesmen's verdicts on each other form one of the features of the book. There are also descriptions of their appearance and character, and the personal assessments of those who knew them well.

These contemporary extracts are followed by the more reflective verdicts of later historians and statesmen, and finally by the views of some historians, English and American, writing at the present time.

Each section has a brief introduction with numbered references to the extracts.

The following general surveys might be used in conjunction with this book.

Robert Blake, *The Conservative Party from Peel to Churchill* (Eyre and Spottiswoode, 1970).
British Prime Ministers [Essays by various authors from History Today] (Allan Wingate, 1953).
Algernon Cecil, *Queen Victoria and her Prime Ministers* (Eyre and Spottiswoode, 1953).

1. Sir Robert Peel, 1788-1850

Did Sir Robert Peel betray the Conservatives over Catholic emancipation and the repeal of the Corn Laws, or did he set his party on a more realistic course? That was the main dispute regarding Peel in his lifetime.

His father, a wealthy, ambitious cotton manufacturer, and a Tory M.P., trained his son for politics from an early age. Peel was a shy and awkward man, but he came into his own in the House of Commons which he dominated for so many years (3). He entered Parliament at the age of 21 and three years later, in 1812, he became Chief Secretary for Ireland, and ten years after that Home Secretary. In both posts he proved himself to be an efficient, hard-working administrator. As Home Secretary he carried out a number of important legal reforms and created the Metropolitan Police Force in 1829—known after him as 'Bobbies' or 'Peelers'.

Peel, however, was no radical. On some issues he was as reactionary as any Tory. For many years he had been one of the main opponents of Catholic emancipation, but the growing unrest in Ireland caused him to change his views.* Irish Protestants received the first hint of this in a speech made by his brother-in-law, George Dawson, in August, 1828 (4–5). In the following year, the Catholic Emancipation Act was passed. Peel strongly defended his change of views, but there was much criticism of him (6–7). His action was soon forgiven, but it was not forgotten. Peel also opposed parliamentary reform (8). Nevertheless, once the 1832 Reform Bill had been passed, he accepted it, and in his address to his constituents in Tamworth in 1834, outlined his new philosophy of conservatism, as he also did at a banquet given in his honour by Conservative M.P.s in 1838 (9–10). Peel held office as Prime Minister for a few months in 1834–5, but it was not until 1841 that he got

* See Nineteenth-century Reformers, Oxford University Press, 1971, pp. 1–14.

back into power again. One of his first actions was to reduce duties on imported corn, but he still remained a supporter of the system of agricultural protection. There was, however, growing pressure from the new manufacturing classes for the repeal of the Corn Laws.* Slowly Peel became convinced that their views were correct. By 1845 there were increasing fears among some Conservatives that he was going to 'betray' them again just as he had done before over Catholic emancipation (11). But there was a large body of middle-class opinion strong in its support for his leadership (12). Peel finally became convinced of the need for repeal and in a speech in May, 1846, strongly defended his new change of view (13). The country gentlemen in the Tory party were incensed and found a brilliant spokesman in Disraeli, who mocked Peel without mercy for this second 'betrayal' (14). The protectionists never forgave Peel and shortly afterwards he was defeated by a combination of Whigs and protectionists and resigned. Peel was pleased to go. He wanted alliances neither with reactionary Tories nor with radicals, but a middle-of-the-road conservatism (15).

Four years later he died, after his horse shied and threw him to the ground (16). There were enthusiastic tributes from the people (17); qualified praise from Disraeli (18); but also criticisms that he had sacrificed principles to expediency (19–20). Later verdicts were more charitable; at least one M.P. saw him as a supreme statesman, though the charge of inconsistency still persisted (21–22). The Earl of Rosebery, who was Liberal Prime Minister from 1894 to 1895, thought correctly that if Peel had not been born into a Tory family, he would have naturally been a Liberal (23). This latter verdict has received even greater support in modern times. The attitudes of present-day historians towards his handling of the Irish question are generally sympathetic (24–26). The charge of betrayal is heard no more; indeed, one of the main authorities on Peel praises him for the consistency of his policy in the last twenty years of his life (27). Other modern historians praise him for what he was once condemned: his reliance on expert advice, his acceptance of the need for reasonable reform, and his adjustments to changing middle-class opinion (28–29).

* See *Nineteenth-century Reformers* (Oxford University Press, 1971), pp. 91–104.

Further Reading

George Kitson Clark, *Peel and the Conservative Party* (Frank Cass, 1964).

Norman Gash, *Mr. Secretary Peel,* The Life of Sir Robert Peel to 1830 (Longmans, 1961).

A. A. W. Ramsay, *Sir Robert Peel* (Constable, 1928).

CHARACTER AND APPEARANCE

Tall and Slender

1 In person he was tall and well formed. His figure, slender rather than robust, made at that time no approach to corpulency. He was active, given to athletic sports; a good walker; fond of shooting, and a good shot . . .

At twenty-one he was attentive to his dress, and dressed well and fashionably . . . It was still the fashion to wear powder in the hair at a dinner or evening party; and this fashion, which concealed the sandy colour of his hair, and suited his complexion, became him well.

Sir Lawrence Peel, *A Sketch of the Life and Character of Sir Robert Peel* (London, 1860).*

A Woman's Walk

2 Sir Robert was tall and well-made, except in his legs, and the defect of those only was that they were too thin, and that, as they tapered much towards the ancle, they seemed too small for the upper man. From some peculiar formation he walked like a woman,—to use a common phrase, he 'sidled' along. . . . [The tones of his voice] were more peculiar than those of any voice I ever heard, either on or off the stage. It combined all the softness and persuasiveness of a woman's with the strength and sonorousness of a man's.

Captain H. Martin, *A Personal Sketch of the late Lamented Sir Robert Peel* (Hamburg, 1850).

'His Two Left Legs'

3 He seems self-assured that he is of importance there [in the

* Sir Lawrence Peel, (1799–1884), a cousin of Sir Robert, and chief justice of Calcutta from 1842 to 1855.

House of Commons]. As he enters at the green door below the bar, and the members, of whatever party, instinctively make way for him, he looks at no one, recognises no one, receives salutation from no one. He seems neither to know or to be known by any member present. He moves straight on, gliding along the floor like something unreal, with steps half-sidling, on what O'Connell called his two left legs, as though he were preparing for the stately minuet. The broad, full frame—tending, of late, to portliness, and looking still more full in the ample vest and long broad-skirted frock-coat—seems almost a weight to its supports: an apprehensive man might fear that the sidling step would weaken into a slight stagger. An air of formality and pre-occupation is on the face. The countenance, though handsome and of fine mould, looks broad, flat,—not open—and traitless. An habitual suppression of feeling has left it without marked features. A complacent gravity alternates with an austere coldness. Or, the brows are elevated with a haughtiness not natural to him; and a strange contradictory smile, sometimes nearly humorous, sometimes almost self-contemning, plays with a slight convulsive motion, as though not quite under control . . .

Arrived at his place, he exchanges no recognitions with his immediate colleagues, but sits apart,—his body prone upon his crossed legs, his hat down upon his ears, his face stretched forward in anxious attention or agitated with nervous twitches, while his right hand, the two fore-fingers forked, strokes slowly down the nose, or plays unconsciously with his seals, or the keys of his despatch-boxes, which lie before him on the speaker's table.

Anon., *Sir Robert Peel as Statesman and Orator* (London, 1846).

CONTEMPORARY VIEWS

Catholic Emancipation

4 Among the distinguished visitors [to a dinner given by Protestants in Derry] was Mr. G. Dawson, brother-in-law of Mr. Peel, member for the county of Londonderry, and Under Secretary of State. This gentleman has long been considered one of the ablest and most determined opponents to the Catholic Claims.

On the above occasion, however, in returning thanks when his health had been drunk, he avowed a change of sentiment— amounting, in fact, to an abandonment of his former principles—which called forth the disapprobation of the company. The Hon. Gentleman observed: 'The state of Ireland is an anomaly in the history of civilised nations—it has no parallel in antient or modern history, and being contrary to the character of all civil institutions, it must terminate in general anarchy and confusion. The peace of Ireland depends not upon the Government, but upon the dictation of the Catholic Association. (*Cries of more's the shame! shame! why not put it down!*) It has defied the Government, and trampled upon the law of the land. There never was a time when the whole Catholic body was so completely roused and engrossed by political passions as at present . . .

There is but one alternative, either to crush the Catholic Association—(*Cheers for several minutes*)—there is but one alternative, either to crush the Catholic Association, or to look at the question with an intention to settle it.'
Gentleman's Magazine, August, 1828.

Secret negotiations

5 Though Mr. Peel's brother-in-law had announced, at a public dinner, his change of opinion, Mr. Peel himself accepted, during the autumn, the public banquets of the gentry and manufacturers of Lancashire, as the champion of the Protestant cause, without allowing a syllable to escape from him, which could raise any suspicion that he was more inclined to surrender the Protestant constitution than he had been three months before. . . .

While the country was thus reposing in secure confidence that the leading members of the government were still faithful to their trust, these very men had determined to go over to the Catholics, and, in secrecy and silence, were arranging their plans to overwhelm every attempt at resistance by the power of ministerial influence. The consent of the king was the first thing to be obtained, and it was likewise the most difficult. His majesty's opinions against the justice and expediency of concession were deeply rooted . . .

Had the people, instead of being lulled into the confidence that those whom they had trusted before, would be trustworthy still, been made aware of the counsels which these very men were pouring into the royal ear, the public voice would have been heard at the foot of the throne, strengthening the deep-rooted convictions of the monarch himself, and the reluctant consent, which was ultimately wrung from him, in all probability, would never have been obtained. When his consent was once obtained, the public voice might be allowed to raise itself without danger; for he then stood pledged to his ministers, if these ministers, by whatever means, could only command a majority in parliament.

The Annual Register, London, 1829.

Peel's Defence

6 Mr. Secretary Peel . . . said . . . that nearly the most painful circumstance that could be imposed on a public man, in the performance of a public duty, must be when, after long acting with a number of individuals,—after proceeding in concurrence with them to the utmost of his power in a particular course of policy, he finds himself called upon, by peculiar circumstances, to separate from them. To separate, he repeated, from men for whose integrity, ability, and conscientious feelings, he entertained, and always should entertain, the profoundest respect, must certainly be counted amongst the severest sacrifices of a public man. But he trusted that his hon. friends would admit this; namely, that his Majesty's ministers stood in a situation different from that in which they were placed: that, in that situation, they had access to information which his hon. friends had not; and above all, that they stood in a peculiar relation to his Majesty, by which they had contracted an obligation, as responsible servants of the Crown, from which they could not relieve themselves by any reference to past declarations or past circumstances, from that duty of giving the best advice which they could form, as to any measure, under the then existing situation of affairs. That was their duty; and whatever might have been the understanding on which governments had been formed, with respect to the Catholic question, and whatever might have been the reservations which individuals had made when entering into the service of the Crown, such understandings and such reservations did not absolve them from the paramount duty of offering the best advice to his Majesty,

upon any important conjuncture, and of being responsible for the consequences of that advice. . . .

The opinions which he had heretofore expressed on the Catholic question he still retained—but he must say, that, looking to the position of the government of the country,—looking to the position of the legislature,—looking to the disunion which had prevailed on this subject in his Majesty's councils,—looking to the disunion which for several years had marked the proceedings of the two branches of the legislature,—and looking to the effect which all these causes had produced on the state of Ireland; considering all these things, he must say, that there appeared to him to be sufficient reasons to induce him to accept of almost any alternative. . . .

His Majesty's ministers were not, and had not been, afraid of the Catholic Association. That intimidation had been resorted to, he readily admitted. But how had it been met? It was put down by the Protestant spirit of the country; and, if it had been continued, his Majesty's ministers were prepared to suppress by the physical force of the country, those offences against the laws which the moral strength of the people should prove unable to subdue . . . He was not a man to yield to intimidation, or to be deterred by threats of commotions; but he could not understand the constitution of that man's mind, who, looking upon Ireland in its present state, could be free from apprehensions of consequences which might arise from allowing such a condition of affairs to continue.

But, the point which weighed most with him in respect to Ireland was this:—he conscientiously believed, that while this disunion existed between the legislative bodies and the government, a proper administration of the law by juries in Ireland was impossible . . .

The conclusion to which he, in conjunction with his friends had arrived, had not been influenced by the recent proceedings of the Catholic Association, nor by the difficulties which might present themselves in once more meeting the parliament. The opinions which he now expressed were formed more than six months ago, almost immediately after the conclusion of the last session. At that time he communicated with his noble friend at the head of his Majesty's government [the Duke of Wellington], and after an attentive consideration of the state of Ireland, they were of opinion, that it was not for the king's service, for the dignity of the Crown, nor for the welfare of the country, that hostility to concessions to the Roman Catholics should still be persisted in. He and his noble friend were of opinion that the time was come for a serious consideration of the question, and that there would be less evil in conceding the question, than in persevering in opposition to it. Placed in this situation, he felt it his first duty to give the best advice to his Majesty; yet, in doing so, he did not forget the peculiar situation in which he stood: he did not forget, that he had for many years past offered, he hoped not a violent nor intemperate, though certainly a steady and unqualified opposition to the claims of the Roman Catholics . . . His opposition had been complete and entire. That opposition, however, had always been confined to that House. He had never exercised it elsewhere.

The Speeches of the late Right Hon. Sir Robert Peel, Bart., delivered in the House of Commons, February 5, 1829 (London, 1853).

Greville's Views

February 6th

7 I was in the House of Commons. Peel was very feeble, and his case for himself poor and ineffective; all he said was true enough, but it was only what had been said to him over and over again for years past, and he did not urge a single argument for acquiescing now which was not equally applicable to his situation two years ago. However, everybody was so glad to have the measure carried that they did not care to attack Peel or his speech . . .

However, thank God, the event is accomplished, no matter how; probably it could not have been done without the concurrence of these Tories, who have, I think, certainly lost their character by their conduct; and there is this evil in the history of the measure, that a blow will have been given to the reputation of public men in general which will, I strongly suspect, have an important though not immediate effect upon the aristocratic influence in this country, and tend remotely to increase the democratic spirit which exists. . . .

To O'Connell and the Association, and those who have fought the battle on both sides of the water, the success of the measure is due. Indeed, Peel said as much, for it was the Clare election which convinced both him and the Duke [of

Wellington] that it must be done, and from that time the only question was whether he should be a party to it or not . . .

February 8th

I dined yesterday with all the Huskissonians at Grant's . . . Huskisson* is in good humour and spirits, but rather bitter; he said that if Peel had asked the advice of a friend what he should do, the advice would have been for his own honour to resign. I said I did not think Peel would have got credit by resigning. He said, 'But don't you think he has quite lost it by staying in?' He owned, however, that the Duke could not have carried it without Peel, that his influence with the Church party is so great that his continuance was indispensable to the Duke.

Charles Greville, *The Greville Memoirs* (ed. Henry Reeve) 4th ed. (Longmans, Green & Co., 1875).**

Opposition to Parliamentary Reform

8 What he was afraid of was, that when the country got a popular parliament, it would jump to conclusions—conclusions that might be right abstractedly, but which, from the great variety of interests they embraced, required the nicest caution and consideration in their management. In the same way with respect to property: he had no fear of its destruction by confiscation; but he was afraid that some popularity-seeking Chancellor of the Exchequer might be forced by a democratic assembly to propose the repeal of taxes, and to adopt steps, the ultimate tendency of which would be, to shake the confidence of the country in the security of property; and that confidence once shaken, there would be an end to the chief stimulus to productive industry, the foundation of all our wealth, power, and eminence . . .

I am satisfied with the constitution under which I have lived hitherto, which I believe is adapted to the wants and habits of the people. I deplore a disposition, which seems too prevalent, to innovate unnecessarily upon all the institutions of the country . . . I will continue my opposition to the last,

* William Huskisson, (1770–1830), who had resigned from the government in 1828 after general disagreements over policy with the Prime Minister, the Duke of Wellington.

** Charles Cavendish Fulke Greville, (1794–1865), clerk to the Privy Council from 1821 to 1859, whose diaries form one of the most important and valuable records of political history in the first half of the nineteenth century.

believing, as I do, that this is the first step, not directly to revolution, but to a series of changes which will affect the property, and totally change the character, of the mixed constitution of this country. I will oppose it to the last, convinced, that though my opposition will be unavailing, it will not be fruitless, because the opposition now made will oppose a bar to further concessions hereafter. If the whole of the House were now to join in giving way, it will have less power to resist future changes. On this ground I take my stand, not opposed to a well-considered reform of any of our institutions which need reform, but opposed to this reform in our constitution, because it tends to root up the feelings of respect, the feelings of habitual reverence and attachment, which are the only sure foundations of government. I will oppose to the last the undue encroachments of that democratic spirit to which we are advised to yield without resistance.

The Speeches of the late Right Hon. Sir Robert Peel, Bart., delivered in the House of Commons, December 17, 1831 (London, 1853).

The Tamworth Manifesto

9 I never will admit that I have been, either before or after the Reform Bill, the defender of abuses, or the enemy of judicious Reforms. I appeal with confidence, in denial of the charge, to the active part I took in the great question of the Currency— in the consolidation and amendment of the Criminal Law— in the revisal of the whole system of Trial by Jury,—to the opinions I have professed, and uniformly acted on, with regard to other branches of the jurisprudence of the country—I appeal to this as a proof, that I have not been disposed to acquiesce in acknowledged evils, either from the mere superstitious reverence for ancient usages, or from the dread of labour or responsibility in the application of a remedy.

But the Reform Bill, it is said, constitutes a new era, and it is the duty of a Minister to declare explicitly—first, whether he will maintain the Bill itself,—and secondly, whether he will act upon the spirit in which it was conceived.

With respect to the Reform Bill itself, I will repeat now the declaration which I made when I entered the House of Commons as a Member of the Reformed Parliament, that I consider the Reform Bill a final and irrevocable settlement of a great constitutional question—a settlement which no friend to the peace and welfare of this country would attempt to disturb, either by direct or insidious means.

Then, as to the spirit of the Reform Bill, and the willingness to adopt and enforce it as a rule of government. If, by adopting the spirit of the Reform Bill, it be meant that we are to live in a perpetual vortex of agitation; that public men can only support themselves in public estimation, by adopting every popular impression of the day—by promising the instant redress of any thing which any body may call an abuse—by abandoning altogether that great aid of Government—more powerful than either law or reason—the respect for ancient rights, and the deference to prescriptive authority,—if this be the spirit of the Reform Bill, I will not undertake to adopt it. But if the spirit of the Reform Bill implies merely, a careful review of institutions, civil and ecclesiastical, undertaken in a friendly temper, combining, with the firm maintenance of established rights, the correction of proved abuses, and the redress of real grievances,—in that case, I can for myself and colleagues undertake to act in such a spirit and with such intentions.

The Address of the Right Hon. Sir Robert Peel, Bart., to the Electors of the Borough of Tamworth (London, 1835).

Conservative Principles

10 Sir Robert PEEL— . . . We feel deeply and intimately that in the union of the conservative party in the country is one of the best guarantees for internal tranquillity and the maintenance of our ancient institutions. . . . By that union we shall best be enabled to maintain the mild predominance of the Protestant faith in this country and in every part of the United Kingdom. By that union we shall be enabled—and by that alone—to promote what we call conservative principles. If you ask me what I mean by conservative principles . . . I will, in conclusion, briefly state what I mean . . . By conservative principles I mean, and I believe you mean, the maintenance of the Peerage and the Monarchy—the continuance of the just powers and attributes of King, Lords, and Commons in this country. By conservative principles I mean, a determination to

resist every encroachment that can curtail the just rights and settled privileges of one or other of those three branches of the state. By conservative principles I mean, that co-existent with equality of civil rights and privileges, there shall be an established religion and imperishable faith, and that that established religion shall maintain the doctrines of the Protestant Church. By conservative principles I mean, a steady resistance to every project which would divert church property from strictly spiritual uses . . .

By conservative principles I mean, a maintenance of the settled institutions of church and state, and I mean also the maintenance, defence, and continuation of those laws, those institutions, that society, and those habits and manners which have contributed to mould and form the character of Englishmen, and enabled this country, in her contests and the fearful rivalry of war, to extort the admiration of the world, and in the useful emulation of peaceful industry, commercial enterprise, and social improvement, have endeared the name of England and Englishmen in every country in the world to those who seek the establishment of liberty without oppression, and the enjoyment of a national and pure form of religion, which is at once the consolation of the virtuous man, and is also the best guarantee which human institutions can afford for civil and religious liberty. (The right honourable baronet then sat down, and the cheering, which had been frequent throughout his speech, was renewed with increased energy and enthusiasm.)

The MARQUIS of CHANDOS next proposed, 'The Army and Navy of the Country'.

General Sir E. KERRISON returned thanks on behalf of the army, and expressed his gratification that the House of Commons had such a leader as the right honourable baronet, and his hope that he and his friends would soon occupy the places of the present ministry; for the sooner these were discharged from office the better.

The Hon. Capt. GORDON returned thanks on behalf of the navy, and said that in whatever situation they were placed they would never suffer political considerations to interfere with the performance of their professional duties, but were always ready to act with fidelity to their Soverign and their country, and one of the highest rewards they could receive was, the approbation of the 313 conservatives now assembled.

LORD STANLEY* rose and said . . . my right hon. friend has truly told you that our union is founded upon higher and more enduring motives. It is founded upon the strongest motives that can actuate private feeling, or influence public conduct. It is founded upon a sense of common danger, and a conviction of common interest; not the sordid, base, personal interest or profit of the individual, but a common conviction impressed upon our minds that danger is threatened to the interests of the country, and that union is the only means by which the danger can be warded off, and our institutions preserved.

The Peel Banquet at Merchant Taylor's Hall, May 12, 1838 (London, 1838).

Dropping the Pilot

11 There is no question which he has handled, on which he has not run us aground. What can we say of our future voyage, when in past times our pilot has so failed us? We once thought this was owing to want of experience, to be corrected by years and adversity. We were wrong. It is owing to the defects of his mind and of his character, *defects which strengthen with years.* His course has been always the same. He fancies that he looks ahead: the truth is, that he sticks to his course till the soundings tell him that he is on the sands; then, in haste and alarm, he throws his cargo in one moment overboard. He took this course on Emancipation. He was the champion of the Protestants; No surrender, was his cry. He stuck to this whilst opinions changed, and objections grew, and he languidly defended a cause which in his soul he had deserted. Then on a sudden loomed the breakers; the Clare election; the terror (quite unfounded) of a disaffected army and an Irish rebellion. Instantly, without a pause, helm about, and the whole cargo, the professions of a life, were cleared at a blow. So it was on Reform: not a point would he concede, not a member to Birmingham, not a representative to Manchester: then, defeated, (for there, it is due to him to say, he met defeat), he made a total change, every principle recast and turned upside down, to suit, as he thinks, a new world.

* Lord Stanley, (1799–1869), later Earl of Derby, who became leader of the Conservative party after the fall of Peel in 1846, and Prime Minister for the first time in 1852.

Look, lastly, at his conduct on the Corn-laws . . . At first, he was the high protectionist; agricultural protection was essential to land, to labour, and to trade. This doctrine he preached from 1815 to 1830, earnestly and loudly . . . In 1837 he was its advocate: he fought the fight in 1838, 1839, and 1840; he clenched it, as we have shown, in 1841. He made a new law of protection in 1842.* Is he the advocate of protection still? Read the speeches which he and Sir James Graham delivered on 10th of June last . . . Read the remarks of the Birmingham meeting delivered whilst we write. What do they all say of Sir Robert Peel's views of protection? That they are gone; that the game is up; that protective duties are to be abandoned. All his arguments that protection was essential to the farmer; that it was needful to be independent of foreign supply; that if we let in cheap corn, worse soils would be abandoned farmers ruined, and labourers expelled; that it was by protection that tillage climbed the hill, and ran into the vale; that from protection arose the smiling hamlet and the thriving farm: all these statements made, dwelt upon, repeated with the dexterity of a first-rate debater and the authority of a party leader, enforced with the utmost seriousness, as if he really felt and believed them, are gone, absolutely gone! . . .

It shows us that the Prime Minister is prepared to throw overboard every principle on pressure; it warns us, that no faith can be placed on his past assurances; that no trust can be reposed in his general principles; that his policy is the work of chance and pressure, and that, if occasion serves, he will give up every institution in England . . . The man who abandons principle, betrays his cause. . . . He says that you must respect existing prejudices, and not shake existing institutions. But there is no such respect. The opponent attacks them with vigour; the leader of the defence is silent; his followers are afraid to speak; the tactique prevails; silence is observed. The public note it. They suppose that laws and institutions which are not defended, have no good defence. Then comes an excitement, and the demand for change: and then the same man who has been silent through cowardice, obeys the calls from terror, declares that the pressure is irresistible, and carries the revolution. And this his friends call wisdom.

J. C. Colquhoun M.P., The Effects of Sir R. Peel's

---

* This was written, of course, before the announcement of the Ministerial Measures of 1846. It was written in November, 1845.

Administration on the Political State and Prospects of
England, in *The English Review*, December, 1845.*

Middle Class Support

12 The question then which presents itself is, whether there is a
prospect, and a rational expectation, not merely of gaining a
temporary victory, but of securing permanently the principle
of protection—of putting a stop to agitation, of persuading the
millions who cry aloud for the abolition of the Corn Laws, to
hold their peace, and to resign themselves to the imposition
of those laws for ever; it is hard to conceive that there can
be one individual not utterly demented, who seriously and
soberly figures to himself the possibility of such a consum-
mation . . . The rapids of Niagara will sooner stand still, than
Corn Law agitation will subside. . . .

If Sir Robert Peel is driven from the helm, the boldest of the
agriculturist champions may well be appalled at the condition
in which such a victory would place the country. They who
think the Corn Laws are the be all and the end all here—
indispensable to us as the air we breathe—that with them we
shall flourish and without them we must decay—may require
no other qualification in a minister than a resolution to maintain these laws: but if all the tried and able men of both the
great parties shall be virtually set aside, and an attempt be
made to put men without experience or reputation in their
places, can it be supposed that the country will tamely endure
such an insane and insulting experiment? The main strength of
Sir Robert Peel consists neither in the support of the
aristocracy nor in any personal popularity; but in the sober
dispassionate opinion of the middle classes that He is the fittest
man to govern the country. There is an immense body of
persons neither Whigs nor Tories, and free from party
prejudices and connections, who, feeling that their own
interests are identified with the prosperity of the country, care
only for having the management of public affairs committed
to the ablest public men. Sir Robert Peel enjoys the reputation
of being sagacious, prudent, and experienced, and therefore
thousands of practical men, who may be indifferent to his
person, and perhaps dislike many of his measures, are well

* John Campbell Colquhoun, (1803–1870), Tory M.P. for Newcastle-under-Lyme,
from 1842 to 1847, and a bitter opponent of Catholic emancipation.

contented to see him the Minister of the Crown. This may not be a glittering, but it is a solid sort of popularity. The same sentiment might possibly be equally satisfied with Lord John Russell and his able colleagues, in whose hands they might consider the interests of the country to be equally secure; but to suppose that the great capitalists and all that mighty mass of industry and intelligence, to whom it is of vital importance that the complicated machinery of government should be skilfully worked—to suppose that they would endure such a government as the Agriculturists could form—a cabinet which would be despised at home and derided abroad, would be the most preposterous delusion that ever entered into the mind of man.

Sir Robert Peel and the Corn Law Crisis (London, 1846), 2nd ed.*

Repeal of the Corn Laws

13 Sir, it is because I cannot with truth allege that if you establish free trade in corn, you will probably become dependent upon foreign nations for your supply of the necessaries of life—it is because I do not believe that the rates of wages vary directly with the price of food—it is because I cannot persuade myself that with respect to the intelligent farmers, it can be considered that this protection is necessary to agricultural prosperity—it is because I cannot establish these facts, I have come to the conclusion that the natural presumption in favour of unrestricted importation ought to prevail, and therefore it is unjust to continue these legislative restrictions upon food . . .

I do believe that, also, by increasing the resources from which you draw your supply of food, by bringing it from the United States, from Odessa, from the Baltic . . . you will receive supplies from so many sources, that dependence on any one nation will be impossible. I cannot contend that the probability of dependence upon foreign nations constitutes a reason for maintaining the Corn-laws. Look now at the different classes of the community. Take, first, the manufacturing population. Is it just towards them to continue these laws? I believe . . . that the great mass of the manufacturing population will be doubly benefited by the removal of these

* This pamphlet was published anonymously by Charles Greville, 1794–1865), the famous political diarist.

PEEL'S CHEAP BREAD SHOP.

OPENED JANUARY 22, 1846.

restrictions; first, by increasing the demand for those manufacturing articles upon which their labour is expended; and,
in the next place, by giving them, from the wages which they
receive, a great command over the necessaries and comforts of
life. . . .

Then, with respect to the agricultural labourer. Can we say
that protection has operated for his advantage? Ireland is
peculiarly agricultural; can it be said that the agricultural
labourer has flourished in Ireland? Is it not the case, that in
the part of the country where the agricultural labourer most
abounds, he has been suffering scarcity and pressure of
hunger? What is the answer made to our statement of the
sufferings of the people of Ireland? 'This is nothing extraordinary—this is nothing unusual—this is nothing out of the
common course of nature; every year this is the same; there
are districts where, every year, the potato crops fail, where
it is impossible to make the two ends meet; the potatoes fail in
June or early in July, and from that time till the new crop is dug
up, the labourer is obliged to subsist upon charity, or whatever
means will suffice for the purpose of maintaining life'. If that
be, as you say, the normal state of the Irish agricultural
labourer—if that be his ordinary condition, and therefore we
are not justified in an extraordinary remedy—can we contend
that protection to agriculture has been greatly for the benefit of
the agricultural classes in Ireland? . . .

With respect to the agricultural class here, I do not deny
that this change in the law will be altogether unaccompanied
by distress. I cannot deny that so great a change can be made
without involving some in distress. I deeply regret it. I wish it
were possible to make any change in any great system of law
without subjecting some persons to distress; but is it not the
fact that the parties who will be most distressed of all, will be
those who have neither science, nor skill, nor capital? Is it
possible permanently to maintain a law which cannot be
shown to be advantageous to the men of science, capital, and
skill, but which can only be maintained in order to give the
means of subsistence to those who have not science, capital
and skill? Should we be justified in maintaining these laws, and
taxing the food of the great body of the community, on the
allegation, not that they are necessary for the protection of
agriculturists who have science and skill, but that they are
necessary for the protection of those who go on adhering to the

old system and have neglected the means of improvement? . . . I believe that the agriculturist with capital and with skill, not only derives no advantage from these laws, but is subject to prejudice on account of them. I believe he has no interest in the maintenance of them . . . I believe it to be of the utmost importance that a territorial aristocracy should be maintained. I believe that in no country is it of more importance than in this, with its ancient constitution, ancient habits, and mixed form of government . . . I believe such an aristocracy to be essential to the purposes of good government. The question only is—what, in a certain state of public opinion, and in a certain position of society, is the most effectual way of maintaining the legitimate influence and authority of a territorial aristocracy? . . . What I doubt is, whether it be the real interest of a territorial aristocracy to attempt to maintain its authority by continuing the restriction on corn. . . . I infer that the privileges of a territorial aristocracy will not be diminished or its influence destroyed by consenting to a free trade in corn, because I firmly believe, speaking generally, that the aristocracy will sustain no injury from it whatever. I do not believe, as I said before, speaking generally, that the value of land, or the privileges of land, or the influence of land, will be diminished . . .

I said long ago, that I thought agricultural prosperity was interwoven with manufacturing prosperity; and depended more on it than on the Corn-laws. Continued reflection has confirmed me in that opinion. I believe that it is for the interest of the agriculturist that you should lay a permanent foundation of manufacturing prosperity; and as your land is necessarily limited in quantity, as your population is increasing, as your wealth is increasing, that the true interests of land are coexistent with the manufacturing and commercial prosperity . . . It is because I believe the interests, direct and indirect, of the manufacturing and agricultural classes to be the same—because I believe they are all interested in the extension of scientific agriculture, that I come to the conclusion that the natural presumption in favour of unrestricted import, ought to prevail.

The Speeches of the late Right Hon. Sir Robert Peel, Bart., delivered in the House of Commons, May 4, 1846 (London, 1853).

Disraeli's Attack

14 We trusted to others (*great cheering*)—to one who by accepting, or rather by seizing that post, obtained the greatest place in the country, and at this moment governs England (*loud cries of 'hear'*). Well, Sir, what happens? The right hon. gentleman, the first minister, told his friends that he had given them very significant hints of the change of his opinions (*laughter*) . . .

Sir, none of the observations of the right hon. gentleman applied to me. More than a year ago I rose in my place and said, that it appeared to me that Protection was in about the same state as Protestantism was in 1828. I remember my friends were very indignant with me for that assertion, but they have been so kind as since to observe that instead of being a calumny it was only a prophecy (*great cheering*). But I am bound to say, from personal experience, that, with the humble exception to which I have referred, I think the right hon. baronet may congratulate himself on his complete success in having entirely deceived his party (*loud and prolonged cheers*). . . .

When the minister at last met the house and his party, he acted as if we had deserted him, instead of his having left us (*great cheering*). Who can forget those tones? Who can forget that indignant glance? . . . which means to say, 'I, a protectionist minister, mean to govern England by the aid of the Anti-Corn-Law League (*cheers*). And, as for the country gentlemen, why, I snap my fingers in their face.' (*continued cheers*). . . .

And now, Sir, I must say, in vindication of the right hon. gentleman (*a laugh*), that I think great injustice has been done to him throughout these debates. A perhaps justifiable misconception has universally prevailed. Sir, the right hon. gentleman has been accused of foregone treachery—of long-meditated deception—of a desire unworthy of a great statesman, even if an unprincipled one—of always having intended to abandon the opinions by professing which he rose to power. Sir, I entirely acquit the right hon. gentleman of any such intention. I do it for this reason: that when I examine the career of this minister, which has now filled a great space in the parliamentary history of this country, I find that for between thirty and forty years . . . that right hon. gentleman has traded on the ideas and intelligence of others (*loud *cheering*). His life has been a great appropriation clause (*shouts of laughter and cheers*). He is a burglar of others' intellect . . . From the days of the Conqueror to the termination of the last reign, there is no statesman who has committed political petty larceny on so great a scale (*renewed laughter*). . . .

Sir, the right hon. gentleman tells us, that he does not feel humiliated. Sir, it is impossible for any one to know what are the feelings of another . . . But this I will tell the right hon. gentleman, that though he may not feel humiliated, his country ought to feel humiliated (*great cheering*). Is it so pleasing to the self-complacency of a great nation, is it so grateful to the pride of England, that one who, from the position he has contrived to occupy, must rank as her foremost citizen, is one of whom it may be said as Dean Swift said of another minister, that 'he is a gentleman who has the perpetual misfortune to be mistaken!' (*great cheering and laughter*) . . .

After the day that the right hon. gentleman made his first exposition of his scheme, a gentleman well known in this house, and learned in all the political secrets behind the scenes, met me, and said, 'Well, what do you think of your chief's plan?' Not knowing exactly what to say; but, taking up a phrase which has been much used in the house, I observed, 'Well, I suppose it's a "great and comprehensive" plan.' 'Oh!' he replied, 'we know all about it! It was offered to us! It is not his plan; it's Popkins's plan!' (*peals of laughter from all parts of the house*). And is England to be governed, and is England to be convulsed, by 'Popkins's* plan?' (*cheers and laughter*). Will he go to the country with it? (*cheers*) . . . Will he go to it with this fantastic scheming of some presumptuous pedant? (*great cheering*). I won't believe it. I have that confidence in the common sense, I will say the common spirit of our countrymen, that I believe they will not long endure this huckstering tyranny of the Treasury bench (*loud cheers*)—these political pedlars that bought their party in the cheapest market, and sold us in the dearest (*enthusiastic cheering*).

The Speech of Mr. Disraeli, delivered in the House of Commons on Friday, May 15, 1846 (London, 1846).

---

* A name presumably invented by Disraeli. In the same year, however, a protectionist pamphlet was published entitled *Popkins' Protest: addressed to the House of Lords*. It is possible that Disraeli got his facts wrong, as he did on other occasions.

Justification of Repeal

15 *Protectionists* indeed!! to close their eyes to the result of every
commercial experiment that has been made—to find every one
of their predictions falsified—to disregard the state of public
opinion—to call the Corn Laws a Labourers' question, and yet
listen to the appalling facts as to the conditions for years past
of the labourers in Dorsetshire and the more purely agricultural
districts—to be willing to encounter the tremendous risk of
two bad harvests and the recurrence of such a state of things
in Paisley and Stockport as was witnessed in the winters of
1841 and 1842—not to see that the Corn Laws would, in such
an event, be swept away with dishonour on the demand of a
starving population—this is to be a *Protectionist!*
*Thank God, I am relieved for ever from the trammels of such
a party! . . .*
I would have dissolved, I would have done anything to carry
the repeal of the Corn Laws . . . But the Corn Laws were
repealed without the necessity for dissolution.
Dissolution after the repeal of the Corn Laws might have
given me a majority. But that majority would have consisted
in great measure of men of democratic principles, approving of
my conduct as to the Corn Laws, sympathising with me on
account of the calumnies and shameful injustice of my
opponents—but with no other bond of political sentiment
between us.
I am a Conservative—the most Conservative act of my life
was that which has caused the sacrifice of power. I was not
prepared to unite with opponents from whom I differ or to
exist as a minister by support on sufferance.
Peel's letter to the Right Hon. John Hope, Lord Justice
Clerk, August 3, 1846, in George Peel ed. *The Private Letters
of Sir Robert Peel* (John Murray, 1920).

A Fatal Fall

16 Sir Robert . . . went out on horseback at about five o'clock,
attended by a groom, for his usual ride . . . Turning up Constitution Hill, nearly opposite the wicket that opens into the
Green Park, he met Miss Ellis, one of Lady Dover's daughters,
who was also on horseback. He advanced to greet her; his
horse made some resistance; it was an eight years' old horse,

which Sir Robert had been riding for about two months. He was gently quieting the animal, when it suddenly shied again, and threw him over its head. He fell violently, with his face to the ground. Two persons who happened to be passing, lifted him up immediately; a physician from Glasgow, Dr. Foucart, who was also near at hand, came up, and asked him if he were hurt. 'Yes, very much,' replied Sir Robert with a deep groan, and before a carriage could be procured, he fainted. Mrs Lucas, who was passing, offered her carriage. . . . The carriage proceeded slowly through the Park to his residence in Whitehall Gardens. . . .

He was carried into the nearest room, the dining room, and laid on a sofa. He never left that room alive, and all movement became so painful to him, that it was with the greatest difficulty he was removed from the sofa to an hydraulic bed, on which he lay in restless agony . . .

All physical pain troubled and agitated him strangely. After his fall, this disturbance, agitation, and aversion to pain, became so strong, that his physicians were unable to succeed in clearly ascertaining all the effects of the accident, and the full extent of the injury. Sir Robert objected to any examination, to any sort of contact; and fell into a state of alarming irritation when his medical attendants insisted . . .

It was not until after the death of Sir Robert Peel, that it was discovered that the fifth rib on the left side was also fractured, and had pressed upon the lung, and produced a congestion of that organ which, it is said, was the determining cause of death.

F. P. G. Guizot, *Memoirs of Sir Robert Peel* (London, 1857).*

The People's Tribute

17   Britannia! Britannia! what makes thee complain
O why so in sorrow relenting
Old England is lost, we are born down in pain
And the nation in grief is lamenting,
That excellent man—the pride of the land,
Whom every virtue possessed him,

* François Pierre Guillaume Guizot, (1787–1874), French historian and statesman, who was Foreign Minister from 1840 to 1847 and Prime Minister from 1847 to the revolution of 1848. He was forced into exile and spent a year in England, before he returned to France.

Has gone to that Home, from whence no one returns,
Our dear friend, Sir Robert, God rest him . . .

Talk of Canning and Pitt for their talents and wit.
And all who upheld that high station,
Oh! there has ne'er been such a noble Premier
As Sir Robert before in the nation,
He'd by no one be led, he'd by no one be said
No Government feared to trust him,
In every way he carried the sway,
For the good of his country, God rest him.
The Death of the Right Hon. Sir Robert Peel, a Song
(London, n.d.).

Disraeli's View of Peel

18 He was gifted with the faculty of method in the highest degree;
and with great powers of application which were sustained by
a prodigious memory . . .

Such a man, under any circumstances and in any sphere of
life, would probably have become remarkable. Ordained from
his youth to be busied with the affairs of a great empire, such
a man, after long years of observation, practice and perpetual
discipline would have become what Sir Robert Peel was in the
latter portion of his life, a transcendent administrator of public
business and a matchless master of debate in a popular
assembly . . .

Thus gifted and thus accomplished, Sir Robert Peel had a
great deficiency; he was without imagination. Wanting
imagination, he wanted prescience. No one was more
sagacious when dealing with the circumstances before him; no
one penetrated the present with more acuteness and accuracy.
His judgment was faultless provided he had not to deal with
the future. Thus it happened through his long career, that
while he always was looked upon as the most prudent and
safest of leaders, he ever, after a protracted display of
admirable tactics, concluded his campaigns by surrendering...

Sir Robert Peel had a peculiarity which is perhaps natural
with men of very great talents who have not the creative
faculty; he had a dangerous sympathy with the creations of
others. Instead of being cold and wary, as was commonly
supposed, he was impulsive and even inclined to rashness . . .

He was ever on the look out for new ideas, and when he embraced them he did so with eagerness and often with precipitancy; he always carried these novel plans to an extent which even their projectors or chief promoters had usually not anticipated . . .

Sir Robert Peel had a bad manner of which he was sensible; he was by nature very shy, but forced early in life into eminent positions, he had formed an artificial manner, haughtily stiff or exuberantly bland, of which generally speaking he could not divest himself. There were however occasions when he did succeed in this, and on these, usually when he was alone with an individual whom he wished to please, his manner was not only unaffectedly cordial but he could even charm. . . . But generally speaking he was never at his ease and never very content except in the House of Commons . . . He had obtained a complete control over his temper which was by nature somewhat fiery. His disposition was good; there was nothing petty about him; he was very free from rancour; he was not only not vindictive, but partly by temperament and still more perhaps by discipline, he was even magnanimous . . .

As an orator Sir Robert Peel had perhaps the most available talent that has ever been brought to bear in the House of Commons. We have mentioned that both in exposition and in reply he was equally eminent . . . In the higher efforts of oratory he was not successful . . . In pathos he was quite deficient; when he attempted to touch the tender passions, it was painful. His face became distorted, like that of a woman who wants to cry but cannot succeed. Orators certainly should not shed tears but there are moments when as the Italians say the voice should weep . . .

One cannot say of Sir Robert Peel, notwithstanding his unrivalled powers of despatching affairs, that he was the greatest minister that this country ever produced, because, twice placed at the helm, and on the second occasion with the court and parliament equally devoted to him, he never could maintain himself in power. Nor, notwithstanding his consummate parliamentary tactics, can he ever be described as the greatest party leader that ever flourished among us, for he contrived to destroy the most compact, powerful and devoted party that ever followed a British statesman. Certainly, notwithstanding his great sway in debate, we cannot recognise him as our greatest orator, for in many of the supreme requisitions of oratory he was singularly deficient. But what he really was, and what posterity will acknowledge him to have been, is the greatest member of parliament that ever lived.

B. Disraeli, *Lord George Bentinck,* A Political Biography (London, 1852).

New style of Leader

19 Sir Robert Peel, in his manly speech on quitting office in 1835 ... said he wished to 'stand well', with the House of Commons. That he has taken pains to do so, shows his sense of the importance of popular approbation. Statesmen, he sees, must now rule through opinion, not as before, through intrigue. He does rule; but as no man ever ruled yet in the Commons House of Parliament. His is not a moral influence, like that of Chatham, or of his gifted son, or Charles James Fox. He is not beloved, esteemed, followed with admiration. His power is solitary, self-created, self-emanating. Napoleon-like, he chose to place the crown on his own head. He is a creature of political isolation. He sees in the House an aggregate meeting of rival interests, always in a state of suppressed hostility on principles, or of open conflict on details. In their mutual jealousy, and consequent weakness, lies his power. He holds the balance. He rules them by their hopes, their fears, their interests; not by their affections or their confidence. But with what exquisite art he conceals his mode of managing them! Knowing that direct dictation would provoke resistance, or humiliating appeals to sordid motives afford a plea for virtuous indignation, how artfully he covers the whole with a varnish of public spirit! At the very moment when appealing the most earnestly to principles, do we find him the most slily addressing himself to interest. Every section, every opinion, and all their possible combinations, are mapped in his mind. Nothing that can win a cheer from any party is rejected ... Under pretence of stopping a gap in the finances, he effected a change of principle from indirect to direct taxation. To reconcile the middle classes to an Income Tax, he let in foreign produce, and promised them cheap provisions. Turning at the same time round to the landed interest, he said: 'Never mind what I say to *them*: no produce to any amount will come in under the Tariff.' In the end, he got increased revenue from both classes; and smiled at the short-sighted

jealousies of those whom he had thus led to do what he believed to be the best for the country. By breaking up the land-marks of party, he does all the work of a coalition. Anon., *Sir Robert Peel as Statesman and Orator* (London, 1846).

An Able Administrator

20 He never originated a single great measure; but no man equalled him in accomplishing them: and he was signally skilled as an administrator. . . . During three-fourths of his life he was the Minister of stationary interests, and therefore the opponent of questions of magnitude, which are essentially questions of progress. The principle of his government was that of expediency . . .

Sir Robert Peel, in the last phase of his changeful life, did some service in shattering the remnants of feudal ascendancy over popular interests and the rightful exercise of public opinion. He was great in demolition. But he failed to reconstruct a new order of government, either from the scattered elements of the great party he overthrew, or from the feebler one which he latterly supported. . . .

It will take perhaps another generation to restore the tone and dignity of statesmanship; and to teach us the truth, that great ministers must be great men.

Though there seldom was less corruption in public men than in these times, there rarely was less confidence in them . . .

Though we are removed from the vices and fatuities of the Liverpool and Newcastle Cabinets . . . we are bereft of the elements of any order of power essential to the fruits of legislation and the functions of Government. This is the natural result of that subjugation of principles to the chances of Parliamentary majorities, of which Sir Robert Peel's career was a type and a sanction. It is the harvest we must expect to reap from the misjudgment which attempts to raise that able administrator, that dexterous debater, and useful man, to a reputation which history and the maturer wisdom of other times will hold sacred to an order of Statesmanship, characterised by the greatness of CHATHAM, the talents of BURKE, and the consistent probity of LANSDOWNE.

Jelinger Symons, *Sir Robert Peel, as a type of Statesmanship* (London, 1856).

LATER ASSESSMENTS

The Best to Come

21 The best of his life might have been to come. He was younger by some years when he died than Palmerston when he won his first great triumph in debate ... It seems likely for many reasons that, if Peel had lived a little longer, he would have been called once again to preside over the councils of his Sovereign ... His intellectual power was at its best when he was suddenly taken from life.

Peel was, undoubtedly, as Lord Beaconsfield has said, a great member of Parliament; but he was surely very much more than that; he was a great statesman, a great Minister ... If we name the best half-dozen of modern English Prime Ministers, we can hardly fail to bring in the name of Peel ... To every difficulty by which he was tried Peel proved himself equal; it was his own proud and honest boast that he had never proposed anything which he did not carry ... It is to his eternal honour that he himself, by the wisdom and the high aim of his policy, helped to consolidate that national prosperity and that popular content whereby some of those dangers were averted which are the ordeal and the touchstone of the supreme order of statesmanship.

Justin McCarthy, M.P., *Sir Robert Peel* (Sampson Low, Marston, Searle & Rivington, London, 1891).*

Secondary Talent

22 Peel's talent, however admirable, was of a secondary order. It was a talent less for creating than for adapting, less for moulding than for regulating, less for discovering than for expounding. With such a talent, he was seldom much before the age or much behind it. He was swift to seize and cunning to execute the ideas floating in the mind of enlightened English society. But he could not construct in imagination the future growth of his own mind or the future course of human history. He lived on the intellectual earnings of his daily toil, but he had no large balance at the bank of thought ... Peel was sagacious, not profound ...

* Justin McCarthy, (1830–1912), journalist, historian and Irish M.P., who succeeded Parnell as chairman of the Home Rule party in 1890.

Scarcely any other English statesman has procured the enactment of so many wise measures. The resumption of cash payments, the amendment of the criminal law, the institution of the Irish constabulary and the London police, Catholic Emancipation, the emancipation of trade, and a crowd of reforms only less beneficial than these, make up a record of useful labour which has seldom been surpassed. Nobody would expect Peel to have done, in addition to his own work, the work of Adam Smith or of Bentham. What matters more is that Peel spent much of his life opposing several of the reforms which he afterwards carried, and that he could not have carried the most important without that power which he had acquired by opposing them. There seems to be little doubt that he was honest in resistance as well as in concession, that in each case he tried to further what he believed to be the public good. But this defence saves his integrity at the expense of his judgment. A man who never modifies an opinion is simply as stupid as he is unteachable. But a man who is always shifting from one opinion to another, lacks something which a man should have . . .

Party government cannot be sound unless parties represent principles, and parties cannot represent principles if the leader will not keep faith with his followers, if he will use to overthrow their principles the power which he derives from them.

F. C. Montague, *Life of Sir Robert Peel* (W. H. Allen, 1888).*

A Natural Liberal

23 But this preparation for politics was not wholly an advantage. It was carried on under the auspices of his father, who called himself a Pittite, when that name was monopolised by High Tories and High Protectionists. Peel, then, found his creed prepared for him without an option. He was sworn to Toryism before he understood the meaning of the oath. This was unfortunate, for Toryism was by no means congenial to the character of his mind. He was a representative of the great middle class, commercially a Liberal, with no aristocratic prejudice or tradition to hamper his examination of any

* Francis Charles Montague, (1858–1935), Professor of History, University College, London, from 1893 to 1927.

question on its merits. His habit of mind would thus, had he been left untrammelled, have made him a Whig, but a Whig who would have developed in the popular direction . . .

He was in 1829 to deal High Toryism an almost mortal blow; to reconstitute a new Toryism by patience and labour; and to shatter all in 1846.

But throughout life there was in him a streak of what we call Liberalism. The inner habit of his mind, though essentially cautious was indeed essentially Liberal.

Lord Rosebery, *Sir Robert Peel* (Cassell & Co., 1899).*

MODERN VIEWS

Achievements in Ireland

24 Peel's over-all approach to the problem of law and order in Ireland presents an excellent case study of the abilities and limitations of the young Tory politician. In his adoption of the preventive principle, of law-enforcement, he was clearly in advance of his time; in his failure to realise that prevention should include efforts to remove the underlying causes of crime, he was a product of his era . . .

Nevertheless, as chief secretary, Peel had given Ireland a police force far superior to any it had possessed in the past, and his police reforms were to have important future significance. The Peace Preservation Force was to serve as the model for future Irish police systems, and the famous Irish constabulary of 1836 is clearly recognisable as its descendant . . . Finally, Peel had helped to prepare the way for future reforms by making the Irish government 'police conscious'. By 1818 the idea of a civil solution to the problems of law and order was firmly established. The military continued to play an important role during periods of widespread disturbance, but where prior to 1815 the government had encouraged the magistrates to rely on military assistance in times of disturbance, Peel's successor was instructed to discourage the practice.

Galen Broeker, 'Robert Peel and the Peace Preservation Force', *The Journal of Modern History* (University of Chicago Press, Illinois, December, 1961).

* Earl of Rosebery, (1847–1929), who served under Gladstone and succeeded him as Prime Minister, 1894–1895. Later he moved increasingly to the right wing of the Liberal party, supporting imperialism and opposing Lloyd George's 1909 Budget.

Catholic Emancipation

25 At the time the main charges against Peel resolved themselves into two: that he changed his mind when he did; and that he had not changed it earlier. On the surface both are easy to refute. To argue, as Knatchbull did, that there was no new threat from Ireland in 1828 that did not exist in earlier years was to ignore the general election of 1826, the growth of the Catholic Association, its alliance with the priesthood and peasantry, and the final challenge of the Clare election. Not Peel alone but the mass of informed and expert opinion in the Irish and English executives held that a potentially revolutionary situation had been created . . . It was also foolish to suggest that Peel should have allowed himself to be converted in 1827 and have assisted Canning in passing emancipation at that date. Then indeed it would have been pertinent to enquire what new lights had dawned upon him; and the inevitable conclusion would have been drawn that he had thrown over his convictions in order to remain in office . . .

Yet behind and perhaps within the unreflecting personal rancour of dull men like Knatchbull and violent men like Wetherell,* there was a real case which Greville** later expressed in more rational and sober language. It was that for fourteen years Peel had led the Protestant party against a host of abler men, and by his personal efforts prolonged a hopeless contest which by reason of its prolongation brought the country at last to the brink of civil war.

Norman Gash, *Mr. Secretary Peel,* The Life of Sir Robert Peel to 1830 (Longmans, 1961).

The Corn Laws and Ireland

26 For some years Peel had been moving slowly towards the belief that the corn laws ought to be repealed, and events in Ireland convinced him that he must act at once. For the irreconcilable protectionists, who comprised a great part of Peel's own party, it was, therefore, a matter of policy to minimise the danger of famine . . . It is to Peel's credit that he did not allow personal or party interests to interfere with his plans for relief.

* Sir Edward Knatchbull, (1781–1849), and Sir Charles Wetherell, (1770–1846), Attorney-General in 1826, reactionary Tory M.Ps. who both strongly opposed Catholic emancipation and other reforms.

** See p. 8.

Early in November 1845 he arranged, on his own responsibility for the purchase by the government of £100,000's worth of Indian corn in the United States, and for its shipment to Cork. It was not his intention that the government should undertake responsibility for feeding the people; but he believed that by selling this grain cheaply it would be possible to keep down the general price of food, and prevent profiteering.

J. C. Beckett, *The Making of Modern Ireland, 1603–1923* (Faber and Faber, 1966).

Peel's Effects on Party

27 The stereotyped conception of Peel as the great party organiser of the thirties will not stand up to detailed examination . . . Peel was not good at handling men, and had notoriously little interest in the humdrum and unelevating details of party management. At no point does he appear to have taken the initiative in improving the purely technical aspects of the party structure . . .

Yet to deny Peel's share in the Conservative recovery after the Reform Act would be absurd. If he contributed little to the technical reforms in the party organisation, he made possibly an even greater contribution to the growth of Conservative feeling in the country at large . . . The aspect of Peel's leadership on which contemporaries laid stress was his success in attracting the moderate 1830 supporters of reform to the cause of Conservatism after 1834 . . . Indeed, the feature of Peel's political philosophy in the last twenty years of his life was its consistency. His tactics varied but his strategic aims were unchanged from 1830 to 1850. Peel believed that there was or had been a British Constitution; he believed that the Reform Act had undermined that constitution; he believed that a constitution issuing in a strong executive was essential to the anarchic age in which he lived . . .

It is difficult not to believe that in the end Peel's sense of his own abilities and of the country's need would have sent him back to office at the head of a union of Whig and Peelite liberals.

Norman Gash, *Peel and the Party System, 1830–50* (Transactions of the Royal Historical Society, 1951) Fifth Series, Vol. 1.

A Good Guide

28 Ever willing to learn from experts, for whom he had a high regard, he was also diligent in un-learning much that he had been taught in his political nursery. He became a good guide just because he changed his mind so frequently, not as a result of meditation on general ideas, or on abstract principles, but because he was confronted throughout his life with what he recognised were fresh issues . . . He accepted the necessity for change in politics, and thereby stood out among European statesmen as an enlightened exponent of progressive and constitutional government. In an age of profound social conflicts and of challenge to all established institutions, he was always ready in the last resort to avoid disorder, conflagration and bloodshed, by accepting *faits accomplis*.

Asa Briggs, 'Sir Robert Peel', in *British Prime Ministers* (Allan Wingate, 1953).

Two-party system

29 The ministry of Peel was in many respects the climax of the long period of Liberal–Tory administrations after 1815; in other respects it was the necessary adjustment of Toryism to the new middle-class ascendancy marked by the great Reform Bill and the other reorganisations of British administration and local government. It introduced a new element of confusion into party politics. Peel was accused of betraying his party over the repeal of the Corn Laws and his other free-trade measures, just as in 1829 he had 'betrayed' it over Catholic emancipation. In fact, after Peel's ministry, both parties accepted the broad principles of the Liberal creed and differed mainly over the speed and methods of their application. It thus became possible to have a real system of party-government, with parties alternating in power without each repealing the measures recently passed by its rival. Without this common ground the working of party-government would have been impossible. Socially it rested on the domination of both parties by the 'middle classes'. Economically it rested on the fact that, although there were great extremes of wealth and poverty, the gap between them was filled by the great extent of the middle classes.

The classical model of solid two-party government did not

appear until the great duel between Gladstone and Disraeli after 1867.

David Thomson, *England in the Nineteenth Century, 1815–1914* (Penguin Books, 1950).

2. Viscount Palmerston, 1784-1865

Was Viscount Palmerston a warmonger, or a tough, but essentially cautious, statesman? Opinions varied greatly in his lifetime and after his death, but in modern times views of him have become increasingly favourable.

Palmerston became a Tory M.P. in 1807 and two years later he was appointed Secretary at War, a post he held until 1828. Although he was a hard-working and efficient administrator, he was better known for his ways with women than his parliamentary skills (1). Under Canning's influence his conservative sympathies lessened and in 1829 he became a Whig. In the following year he was appointed Foreign Secretary, remaining in that post for the next eleven years, apart from a few months when Peel was in power (7). His publicly-stated policy was to preserve peace so that commerce could flourish, to make Britain's voice heard abroad, and to support national independence movements (8–11). In private, however, he openly admitted the need to bully smaller powers, as a note to Sir George Bonham, the Governor of Hong Kong, makes clear (12).

The most notorious case of Palmerston's gun-boat diplomacy occurred over Don Pacifico, a Portuguese money-lender, who claimed to be British because he had been born in Gibraltar. Palmerston ordered Greek shipping to be seized in support of his exaggerated claim for £31,000 compensation against the Greek government. Palmerston's action was strongly attacked by Lord Stanley (later Earl of Derby, the Conservative prime minister) in the House of Lords, which passed a critical motion (13). He was also attacked by many M.P.s, including Gladstone.* But Palmerston, in one of his greatest and longest speeches, which lasted nearly five hours, fought back and succeeded in winning the support of the House of Commons (14). His declaration that Britons had the

* See pp. 117–8.

right to be protected by their government wherever they might be led to other similar claims against foreign governments (15).

The increasing individualism of his views, like his support for Napoleon III's *coup* in 1851, caused conflicts with his colleagues and with Queen Victoria (16). Palmerston was dismissed by Lord John Russell, the prime minister, in December, 1851. But his views were so popular among many middle-class people that he could not be excluded from office for long. In the following year Lord Aberdeen appointed Lord Palmerston Home Secretary. In 1853 Palmerston resigned, but he withdrew his resignation after a few days. Karl Marx, one of the bitterest opponents of Palmerston—whom he once called 'that brilliant boggler and loquacious humbug'—thought Palmerston had resigned merely in an attempt to increase his own popularity (17).

After the start of the Crimean War there were increasing public demands for Palmerston to be made premier. These demands were strongly opposed by a powerful group of propagandists who firmly believed that Palmerston was pro-Russian (18). But Lord Aberdeen's leadership was so ineffectual, and the war was going so badly, that in 1855, the Queen, with some reluctance, appointed Palmerston prime minister for the first time—at the age of seventy (19). He brought the war to a successful conclusion and, apart from the brief Derby ministry of 1858–1859, remained prime minister for the rest of his life, dominating parliament and blocking many much-needed reforms, which were not introduced until Gladstone became premier in 1868.

Palmerston died on October 18, 1865—two days before his eighty-first birthday—retaining his physical courage and his capacity for hard work to the last (20–21). *The Times* said, correctly, that the death of this 'truest Englishman' marked the end of an epoch (22). Talleyrand, the French statesman, thought he was probably the most able statesman he had ever met (23). Some commentators, like Richard Holt Hutton, editor of the *Spectator,* had by that time rejected the earlier, general view that he was rash and hot-headed (24). Nevertheless this critical view persisted long after his death and even now there are some historians who see him as an essentially limited, power-seeking individual (25–26). But the consensus among historians now is that he was a prudent statesman, intent on preserving peace—with a modern statesman's ability to manipulate the Press (27–29). History has tended to justify Palmerston's own views of himself and his policies.

Further Reading

Jasper Ridley, *Lord Palmerston* (Constable, 1970).
Donald Southgate, *The Most English Minister* (Macmillan, 1966).

CHARACTER AND APPEARANCE

Mr. Cupid

1 Of Lord PALMERSTON, Foreign Secretary, and member for Tiverton, I have but little to say. The situation he fills in the Cabinet gives him a certain degree of prominence in the eyes of the country, which he certainly does not possess in Parliament. His talents are by no means of a high order. . . . He is an indifferent speaker. I have sometimes seen him acquit himself, when addressing the House, in a very creditable manner; but he often stutters and stammers to a very unpleasant extent, and makes altogether an indifferent exhibition. His voice is clear and strong, but has a degree of harshness about it which makes it grate on the ear . . .

In person, Lord Palmerston is tall and handsome. His face is round, and is of a darkish hue. His hair is black, and always exhibits proofs of the skill and attention of the *perruquier*.* His clothes are in the extreme of fashion. He is very vain of his personal appearance, and is generally supposed to devote more of his time in sacrificing to the Graces** than is consistent with the duties of a person who has so much to do with the destinies of Europe. Hence it is that *The Times* newspaper has fastened on him the *soubriquet* of Cupid. He is about forty-five years of age.

James Grant, *Random Recollections of the House of Commons* (London, 1836).***

---

* wig-maker.
** the three beautiful goddess sisters of Greek mythology: a reference to Palmerston's notorious amorous adventures.
*** James Grant, (1802–1879), journalist and editor of the *Morning Advertiser* from 1850 to 1871.

Foreign Office Views

2 George Villiers is at last acknowledged Minister to Madrid. He told me he was with Palmerston at his house yesterday morning, and was much struck with his custom of receiving all his numerous visitors and applicants in the order in which they arrive, be their rank what it may . . .

The other night I met some clerks in the Foreign Office to whom the very name of Palmerston is hateful, but I was surprised to hear them . . . give ample testimony to his abilities. They said that he wrote admirably, and could express himself perfectly in French, very sufficiently in Italian, and understood German; that his diligence and attention were unwearied—he read everything and wrote an immense quantity; that the foreign Ministers (who detest him) did him justice as an excellent man of business. His great fault is want of punctuality, and never caring for an engagement if it did not suit him, keeping everybody waiting for hours on his pleasure or caprice.

Charles Greville, *The Greville Memoirs,* ed. Henry Reeve (Longmans, Green, 1875).

Hard Worker

3 Lord Palmerston himself had no leisure for social duties. His day was so occupied when Parliament was sitting, that he was accustomed to take only one meal. He rose at about nine o'clock, worked in his study till nearly noon, then drove to Downing Street, where he gave audiences, received his colleagues, and presided at Cabinet Councils, and afterwards, from four o'clock in the afternoon, often sat for twelve consecutive hours in the House of Commons. As leader of the House he was obliged always to be on the spot to answer questions and conduct the debate. At night, often in the early morning hours, the old gentleman would trudge home on foot, a half hour's walk, to breathe some fresh air after the heated atmosphere of the House. Nor did he rest at once when reaching home, for he never omitted, before going to bed, to write down with his own hand the usual report of the last sitting. This report had always to lie the next morning on the Queen's breakfast table. It was to the Prime Minister's interest to forestall the newspapers, and submit to the Queen without

delay his own views about the proceedings of Parliament.
Lady Palmerston spoke to me once about this unavoidable
hardship in official life, and added naively, 'I would far rather
that my husband were only Foreign Minister or Home
Secretary, for since he is become Prime Minister I see nothing
of him. He never comes to bed till four or five o'clock . . .'
Count Charles Frederick Vitzthum, *St. Petersburg and
London in the years 1852–1864*, ed. Henry Reeve (Longmans,
Green, 1887).*

Poor Speaker

4 I must say a word about Lord Palmerston, who was born in
1784, entered Parliament in 1807, and was still leading the
House of Commons when I first attended its debates. A man
who, when turned seventy, could speak from the 'dusk of a
summer evening to the dawn of a summer morning' in
defence of his foreign policy, and carry the vindication of it by
a majority of 46, was certainly no common performer on the
parliamentary stage; and yet Lord Palmerston had very
slender claims to the title of an orator. His style was not only
devoid of ornament and rhetorical device, but it was slipshod
and untidy in the last degree. He eked out his sentences with
'hum' and 'hah'; he cleared his throat and flourished his
pocket-handkerchief . . . ; he rounded his periods with 'you
know what I mean' and 'all that kind of thing' and seemed
actually to revel in an anti-climax . . . It taxed all the skill of
the reporters' gallery to trim his speeches into decent form;
and yet no one was listened to with keener interest, no one
was so much dreaded as an opponent, and no one ever
approached him in the art of putting a plausible face upon a
doubtful policy and making the worse appear the better cause.
Palmerston's parliamentary success perfectly illustrates the
judgment of Demosthenes,** that 'it is not the orator's
language that matters, not the tone of his voice; but what
matters is that he should have the same predilections as the
majority, and should entertain the same likes and dislikes as

*Count Charles Frederick Vitzthum von Eckstaedt, the long-serving envoy of
Saxony in London, who was said to know more diplomatic secrets than anyone else
at that time.
** The famous Athenian orator of the third century B.C., judged to be one of the
greatest of all times.

his country'. If those are the requisites of public speaking, Palmerston was supreme.

George W. E. Russell, *Collections and Recollections* (Thomas Nelson & Sons, n.d.).*

Appearance in Old Age

5 Some of us . . . may have seen him rise quickly and lightly, when near fourscore, from his seat in the House of Commons, and speak with clearness and directness, but with no attempt at eloquence, and often with some hesitation, at the table; his black frock-coat buttoned across the well-knit and erect figure of middle stature, his sentences spoken towards the bar of the House; his grey short hair brushed forward, and the grey whiskers framing the head, erect on the shoulders. Some may remember, under the shaven chin, the loose bow-knot, neatly tied, at the throat, the bit of open shirt-front with short standing collars. Some . . . may have looked up at that refined and resolute face, and, with the irreverence of youth, have noticed that the whiskers were much greyer closer to the cheek, and that the darker hue that pervaded them was not the result either of old age or of early nature. Some may have attended his last receptions at Cambridge House, that handsome white building standing a little retired from Piccadilly, to which its court opens by two wide entrances. There they may have been charmed with the oldfashioned and frank courtesy that bade them welcome as soon as they had reached the centre room at the stair top, which was the place at which the firm figure of the old statesman, clad in well-made evening dress and very neat polished boots, met them and gave them a hearty shake of the hand, as they passed on to be greeted with equal courtesy by Lady Palmerston. But age was telling in those days even on her husband, and he used to forget whom he had greeted, and repeat the kindly handshake twice or even thrice.

Marquis of Lorne, *Viscount Palmerston* (Sampson Low, Marston & Co., 1892).**

* George William Erskine Russell, (1853–1919), author, Liberal M.P., Under-Secretary of State for India, 1892–1894.
** Marquis of Lorne, 9th Duke of Argyll, (1845–1914), Unionist M.P. and Governor-General of Canada (1878–1883). Married Princess Louise, Victoria's daughter, 1871.

Cambridge House Receptions

6 Palmerston was as full of loving attentions to his wife* as the youngest lover. She was at once a mother and wife in her care of him. He never knew whether he should dine at home or not. She looked after everything. She generally held her receptions during the season on Saturday evenings. Although the old lady could command the services of sons and daughters, grandsons and granddaughters, she herself always added with trembling hand the name of the invited guest to the printed form, 'Lady Palmerston at home'. The best society was to be met at her receptions, and they were much in request. Woe to the member of his own party who had spoken or voted against Lord Palmerston in the House; he was unrelentingly punished by receiving no invitation; nor was his name replaced on the list till he had thought better of his disobedience.

Lady Palmerston's dinners were excellent, and rivalled those of Rothschild. Only you had to beware of going there too early, as you ran the risk in that case of finding neither the master nor the mistress of the house in the drawing room. Once on entering the house at half-past eight o'clock, I met Lord Palmerston just going out for a ride before dinner on his old grey horse in Rotten Row. This grey horse, familiar to all Londoners, was the despair of the old lady, for she herself had four grey carriage horses, and feared lest people should think that her husband rode one of them.

Count Charles Frederick Vitzthum, *St. Petersburg and London in the years 1852-1864,* ed. Henry Reeve (Longmans, Green, 1887).

CONTEMPORARY VIEWS

Long Apprenticeship

7 The minister who now assumed the responsibility of Foreign Affairs, and who has been for twenty-five years prominently before the world, had served such an apprenticeship to the business of administration as perhaps no other statesman had ever passed through . . . Though an Irish peer, Lord Palmerston had not many powerful friends to push him over

---

* In December, 1839, at the age of fifty-five, he married Lady Cowper, sister of Lord

many of the notable political, literary and social figures of the day.

the heads of able rivals. He owed his appointment to the important post of Secretary at War entirely to the reputation which he so early acquired. For nearly twenty years he performed the duties of that department with such efficiency and success as may perhaps have been equalled, but have certainly never been surpassed. He was not the slave of routine, but a zealous administrative reformer. The intricate details of military finance, and the regulations of the army were subjected to his careful supervision; and immense improvements were effected, for which he neither received nor expected popular applause. Few people but those intimately conversant with this department, ever knew how much Lord Palmerston had done for the efficiency of the service, or even had the least idea of his great administrative abilities. When he entered the War Office he found everything in the greatest confusion; but after his long tenure of this important place he left it a model of order and industry . . .

When Canning became Foreign Minister, Lord Palmerston's consciousness of his great abilities slowly awakened. He gradually overcame what must be called, however surprising it may seem, his habitual modesty. He spoke well on the affairs of Spain. He spoke well and more frequently on other topics. He began to announce some decided opinions on the political and commercial questions of the day. For Mr. Canning he now felt warm admiration, and adhered to him with generous fidelity when this . . . statesman formed his ministry, and so many influential Tory politicians sent in their resignations and positively refused to serve under a Prime Minister favourable to the claims of the Roman Catholics.

Thomas MacKnight, *Thirty Years of Foreign Policy* (London, 1855).

Foreign Policy

8 Sir, when upon former occasions, I have felt it my duty to bring under the consideration of the House, the foreign policy of his Majesty's Ministers, and to point out, what I think, the false and injurious principles upon which they have acted; my right hon. friends, for want perhaps of better arguments to assail me with, have endeavoured to put me down with a cry; and one and all have exclaimed to the House, 'Listen not to him, for he would involve you in war.'. . .

Sir, I deny the charge, both in argument and in fact. I say that war is neither the object of my wish, nor would have been the consequence of the measures which I would have advised . . . I am neither mad, nor destitute of ordinary sense; how then is it possible, I could plunge my country into unnecessary war?

Lord Palmerston, House of Commons, March 10, 1830 (Hansard, 1830).*

9 The Ministers had been accused of favouring revolution. That accusation was entirely unfounded and unjust. They had, indeed, given their moral support to the great Spanish nation, which was endeavouring, of its own accord, to improve its institutions, and to imitate the proud example of this country, by obtaining the inestimable privilege of a representative Government . . . They might boast, that during the period they had been responsible for the conduct of the affairs of this country the people of Belgium had become free, independent, prosperous, and tranquil. That Portugal, which had been worse governed than Spain, whose great natural resources were entirely crushed and rendered unavailing by a long continued system of misgovernment—that Portugal had at last established a free constitution, and was ready to profit by her alliance with this country and Spain . . . He might be allowed to hope that Spain might yet follow the example set by Belgium and Portugal, and that she might become, with the assistance of England, what she was in former times, a great and powerful member of the European community . . . If he could claim any part, however humble, in such a triumph he should feel it a high honour, and should find in it a source of proud satisfaction to the latest hour of his life.

Lord Palmerston, House of Commons, March 10, 1837 (Hansard, 1837).**

* In the 1830s Palmerston tried to establish a block of constitutional Governments in the Iberian peninsula by supporting the young queens of Portugal and Spain against the reactionary pretenders to the throne. Palmerston's plea that the British should help to expel Dom Miguel, who had usurped the Portuguese throne in 1828, led to accusations that he was a warmonger.

** Palmerston's support of the legitimate governments of Spain and Portugal had only a limited success. Although the Portuguese pretender was expelled in 1834 and the Spanish pretender, Don Carlos, in 1837, corruption and disorders continued, particularly in Spain, for many years afterwards. Palmerston's support of Belgium, which revolted against Dutch rule in 1830 and established a kingdom under Leopold of Saxe-Coburg-Gotha, was more successful in helping to establish a constitutional monarchy.

10 But all I say is that our guiding rule is to promote and advance, as far as we can, the interests of the country to which we have the good fortune to belong, and which we have the honour to serve. We have no everlasting union with this or that country—no identification of policy with another. We have no natural enemies—no perpetual friends. When we find a Power pursuing that course of policy which we wish also to promote, that Power, for the time, becomes our ally; and when we find a country whose interests are at variance with our own, we are involved for a time with the Government of that country. We find no fault with other nations for pursuing their interests; and they ought not to find fault with us if, in pursuing our interests, our course may be different from theirs.
   Lord Palmerston, House of Commons, May 16, 1848 (Hansard, 1848).*

11 It is most desirable that foreign nations should know that, on the one hand, England is sincerely desirous to preserve and maintain peace—that we entertain no feelings of hostility towards any nation in the world—that we wish to be on the most friendly footing with all—that we have a deep interest in the preservation of peace, because we are desirous to carry on with advantage those innocent and peaceful relations of commerce that we know must be injured by the interruption of our friendly relations with other countries: but, on the other hand, it is also essential for the attainment of that object, and even essential for the protection of that commerce to which we attach so much importance, that it should be known and well understood by every nation on the face of the earth that we are not disposed to submit to wrong, and that the maintenance of peace on our part is subject to the indispensable condition that all countries shall respect our honour and our dignity, and shall not inflict any injury upon our interests. . . . I agree with those who think—and I know there are many in this country who entertain the opinion—that there are two objects which England ought peculiarly to aim at. One is to maintain peace; the other is to count for something in the transactions of the world—that it is not fitting that a country occupying such a proud position as England—that a country having such

* During 1848 Palmerston had constantly to defend himself against charges made by the pro-Turkish lobby, led by a former diplomat and M.P., David Urquhart, that his policies favoured Russia. Urquhart persistently urged parliament to investigate Palmerston's conduct of foreign affairs with a view to his impeachment for treason.

various and extensive interests, should lock herself up in a simple regard to her own internal affairs, and should be a passive and mute spectator of everything that is going on around.

It is quite true that it may be said, 'Your opinions are but opinions, and you express them against our opinions, who have at our command large armies to back them—what are opinions against armies?' Sir, my answer is, opinions are stronger than armies. Opinions, if they are founded in truth and justice, will in the end prevail against the bayonets of infantry, the fire of artillery, and the charges of cavalry . . . Why, for a great many years the Governments of Europe imagined that they could keep down opinion by force of arms, and that by obstructing progressive improvement they would prevent that extremity of revolution which was the object of their constant dread. We gave an opinion to the contrary effect, and we have been blamed for it. We have been accused of meddling with matters that did not concern us, and of affronting nations and Governments by giving our opinion as to what was likely to happen; but the result has proved, that if our opinions had been acted upon, great calamities would have been avoided . . . Those Governments, those Powers of Europe, have at last learned the truth of the opinions expressed by Mr. Canning, 'That those who have checked improvement because it is innovation, will one day or other be compelled to accept innovation when it has ceased to be improvement'.

I say, then, it is our duty not to remain passive spectators of events that in their immediate consequence affect other countries, but which in their remote and certain consequences are sure to come back with disastrous effect upon us; that, so far as the courtesies of international intercourse may permit us to do, it is our duty, especially when our opinion is asked, as it has been on many occasions on which we have been blamed for giving it, to state our opinions, founded on the experience of this country—an experience that might have been, and ought to have been, an example to less fortunate countries. At the same time, I am quite ready to admit that interference ought not to be carried to the extent of endangering our relations with other countries.

Lord Palmerston, House of Commons, July, 21, 1849 (Hansard, London 1849).*

* Palmerston's sympathies lay with the Hungarian nationalists, led by Lajos

Principles and Practice

12 'The Time is fast coming when we shall be obliged to strike another Blow in China . . . These half-civilised Governments such as those of China, Portugal, Spanish America, all require a dressing every eight or ten years to keep them in order. Their minds are too shallow to receive an Impression that will last longer than some such Period and warning is of little use. They care little for words and they must not only see the Stick but actually feel it on their Shoulders before they yield to that only argument which to them brings conviction . . .

'Palmerston autograph note, September 29, 1850, to Sir George Bonham',* quoted in W. C. Costin, *Great Britian and China, 1833–1860* (Oxford University Press, 1937).

Don Pacifico: Lord Stanley's View

13 It seems that the Athenian mob take great delight on Easter Sunday in burning a representation of Judas Iscariot; but on Easter Sunday, 1847, in consequence of the presence in Athens of the Baron C. M. de Rothschild, the Government, out of compliment to that gentleman, took measures to prevent the assembling of the people . . . An opinion arose, however, that M. Pacifico had obtained the discontinuance of this annual celebration, and a mob assembled, and, most indefensibly, made an attack upon M. Pacifico's house and destroyed what furniture there was in it, and, indeed, according to his statement, everything else . . . I think that circumstance gives to M. Pacifico a fair and reasonable claim to compensation for those injuries which he sustained in property or person, and which the Greek Government were unable or unwilling to prevent. But when we come to look at M. Pacifico's bill of costs, it is really one which passes credibility. . . .

My Lords, I have said that, according to the statement of M. Pacifico, every article of his furniture was absolutely demolished or carried away, not a vestige left behind, except a

Kossuth, in their revolt against Austrian rule in 1848, but he refused to give them practical support as he believed that a strong Austro-Hungarian empire was necessary to maintain stability in Europe.

Governor of Hongkong in 1847. After the Chinese authorities had seized a British cargo of opium in 1839, Britain fought the so-called Opium War against China. Under the Treaty of Nanking, 1842, China was forced to pay an indemnity, to open some ports to trade and to cede Hongkong to the British.

basin full of broken crockery, and a single sheet of extra-ordinary fineness, which fortunately was left to prove the quality of its companions . . . My Lords, no upholsterer's catalogue can be more complete than that which occupies some pages of the blue book on your Lordships' table, enumerating in the minutest detail, every article in M. Pacifico's house, from the sofas and chairs in the drawing room, to the stew pans, the jelly moulds, the skimming ladles in the kitchen . . . Then the description of the furniture! Why, the house of this M. Pacifico, this petty usurer, who, as I have said, was trading on a borrowed capital of £30, is represented to have been furnished as luxuriously as it might have been if he had been another Aladdin with full command of the Genii of the ring and of the lamp . . . I doubt if many of your Lordships have in your houses (I am sure I have not in mine) furniture of this gorgeous description . . .

When the demand [for compensation] was made at Athens in January, 1850, it was required that all claims that had been sent into the Greek Government, just or unjust, should be paid in full, with interest, within the period of twenty-four hours . . . It was in support of the exaggerated pretensions of M. Pacifico . . . that a British fleet was sent to demand compliance with an unreasonable request in twenty-four hours, and on failure of compliance to capture the vessels of a friendly power, and to punish, not alone the sovereign, but the people and their commerce . . . The vessels of the Greek State were, in the first place, seized by our ships, and when these were found insufficient to meet the demand—and mark, insufficient to meet the demand only because that demand comprised the whole amount of Pacifico's preposterous claim—an embargo was laid upon private vessels, and private commerce and private interests were interfered with, in the expectation that, by the pressure of distress upon their commerce, the determin-ation of the Greek Government and the Greek people would be broken, and that the full amount of the demand would be conceded . . . Let me here observe that the Greek people nobly sustained the protest which their Minister had delivered in their name, so that, if the idea of the noble Viscount [Palmerston] was to effect his object by quelling the spirit of the Greek people, that object utterly failed: the sense of oppres-sion rallied round the King of Greece, not only the sympathies of Europe, but the earnest zeal of his own people . . .

I am bound to say, strongly as I disapprove of the course of our Government in the matter, that I do not find Sir W. Parker,* or any of the officers engaged in executing these orders, overstepped in the slightest degree the letter of their instructions . . . And I believe I am only doing bare justice to the distinguished officer I have named, and to the officers acting under him, when I express the belief that they would, one and all, rather have been engaged in deadly conflict with the fiercest enemy this country ever encountered, than have seen the honour of the British flag thus prostituted by attacking a weak, unoffending people, interrupting harmless commerce, and plundering wretched, half-pauper fishermen of their sole means of subsistence.

Let me now advert to the effect which this step—this violent step—is calculated to have upon our relations with foreign Powers. I need only ask your Lordships to look at the papers on the table to satisfy yourselves what that effect has already been. In the very first instance, Baron Brunnow, the Russian Minister at St. James's, felt it to be his duty to call upon Lord Palmerston for an explanation of the course the noble Viscount proposed to take with Greece . . . The despatch of the 19th February, 1850, was addressed by the Russian Minister to Lord Palmerston, couched in language which I will not distress your Lordships by repeating; language which it must be deeply painful to a British subject to read as addressed to a British Minister, but doubly painful when he reflects that, bitter, imperious, offensive as the language is, it is no more bitter, more imperious, more offensive, than the occasion justified. The Russian Minister did not deny that England had claims upon Greece, but he contended, most justly, considering the relations in which France and Russia stood towards Greece, that, before extreme measures were adopted by England, some intimation at least was due to Powers equally with herself concerned in maintaining the independence of the weaker Power.

Lord Stanley, House of Lords, June 17, 1850 (Hansard, 1850).**

* Sir William Parker, (1781–1866), Commander-in-Chief during the latter part of the war against China, 1839–1842. He was appointed Admiral of the Fleet in 1863.

** Lord Stanley, (1799–1869), 14th Earl of Derby, 1851, who held office as Conservative prime minister for three short periods, being succeeded by Disraeli in February, 1868.

Palmerston's Defence

14 Now, the resolution of the House of Lords involves the future as well as the past. It lays down for the future a principle of national policy, which I consider totally incompatible with the interests, with the rights, with the honour, and with the dignity of the country; and at variance with the practice, not only of this, but of all other civilised countries in the world . . . The country is told that British subjects in foreign lands are entitled . . . to nothing but the protection of the laws and the tribunals of the land in which they happen to reside. The country is told that British subjects abroad must not look to their own country for protection, but must trust to that indifferent justice which they may happen to receive at the hands of the Government and tribunals of the country in which they may be . . .

Now, I deny that proposition; and I say it is a doctrine on which no British Minister ever yet has acted, and on which the people of England never will suffer any British Minister to act . . . We shall be told, perhaps, as we have already been told, that if the people of the country are liable to have heavy stones placed upon their breasts, and police-officers to dance upon them; if they are liable to have their heads tied to their knees, and to be left for hours in that state; or to be swung like a pendulum, and to be bastinadoed* as they swing, foreigners have no right to be better treated than the natives, and have no business to complain if the same things are practised upon them. We may be told this, but that is not my opinion, nor do I believe it is the opinion of any reasonable man . . .

M. Pacifico having, from year to year, been treated either with answers wholly unsatisfactory, or with a positive refusal, or with pertinacious silence, it came at last to this, either that his demand was to be abandoned altogether, or that, in pursuance of the notice we had given the Greek Government a year or two before, we were to proceed to use our own means of enforcing the claim. 'Oh! but,' it is said, 'what an ungenerous proceeding to employ so large a force against so small a Power!' Does the smallness of a country justify the magnitude of its evil acts? Is it to be held that if your subjects suffer violence, outrage, plunder in a country which is small and weak, you are to tell them when they apply for redress, that the country is so weak and so small that we cannot ask it for compensation? . . .

* caned on the soles of the feet.

I therefore fearlessly challenge the verdict which this House, as representing a political, a commercial, a constitutional country, is to give on the question now brought before it; whether the principles on which the foreign policy of Her Majesty's Government has been conducted, and the sense of duty which has led us to think ourselves bound to afford protection to our fellow-subjects abroad, are proper and fitting guides for those who are charged with the Government of England; and whether, as the Roman, in days of old, held himself free from indignity, when he could say *'Civis Romanus sum'*; so also a British subject, in whatever land he may be, shall feel confident that the watchful eye and the strong arm of England, will protect him against injustice and wrong.

Lord Palmerston, June 25, 1850 (Hansard, 1850).*

'Civis Romanus' and its Effects

May 28th, 1852
I fear this business of Mr. Mather at Florence will give me a great deal of trouble, as Mather *père* is furious at only obtaining £250 for the injury done to his son's head, his first demand being £5,000. The latter gentleman chose to stand in the way of a body of Austrian soldiers marching through the street with their band, and refused to move, on which the officer commanding struck him with his sword, and cut his head open, though not dangerously . . . The Opposition, in view of the coming elections, are making capital of this and other freaks of travelling Englishmen who get themselves into scrapes abroad, and, being often deservedly punished or arrested, call upon their Government for protection. This conduct on their part is very much due to a blustering speech made some time ago by Lord Palmerston, declaring that John Bull, wherever he was, or whatever he did, was to be as sacred as the ancient 'civis Romanus'.

Earl of Malmesbury, *Memoirs of an Ex-Minister* (Longmans, Green, 1885).**

Russell Sacks Palmerston

16 At the close of the year [1851] the French *coup d'état* led,

* For Gladstone's speech in the same debate see pp. 117–8.
** Earl of Malmesbury, (1807–1889), Foreign Secretary in the short-lived Derby administration of 1852.

among further consequences, to the remarkable episode of Lord Palmerston's dismissal.

A certain antagonism had long existed between Palmerston and the Prince Consort. The Prince could not approve of the restless, interfering, and demonstrative line of policy which the Minister since 1848 had adopted more and more, which offended the Continental Governments, injured England, and benefited nobody. The Prince stood up for the right of supervision and control belonging to the Crown in foreign politics. This was again displeasing to the self-willed Lord, and the means and artifices he employed to escape from that control did not improve matters. On the other hand, since the Greek Dom Pacifico affair in 1850, and his expressions of sympathy for Kossuth* and the defeated chiefs on the Continent, Palmerston had become burdensome to his own colleagues.

As early as November Stockmar wrote, 'I think the man has been for some time insane'.

He says in a letter of December 22, 'Ever since I returned here, therefore for the last two months, he has been guilty of follies, which confirm me more and more in my former opinion, that he is not quite right in the mind. The Prince might have felt strongly tempted to rush in and throw him over, but he quite agreed with my advice, which was that he ought to remain a mere spectator, as I feel certain that, if Palmerston requires another thrust, his colleagues themselves will give it.'. . . .

As early as August, 1850, the Queen had sent a memorandum to the Prime Minister, Lord John Russell, in which she expressed distinct demands with regard to Lord Palmerston's mode of conducting business; and from this we gather indirectly, what the Queen till then had had to complain of. The memorandum says, 'The Queen requires, first, that Lord Palmerston will distinctly state what he proposes in a given case, in order that the Queen may know as distinctly to what she is giving her Royal sanction. Secondly, having once given her sanction to a measure, that it be not arbitrarily altered or modified by the Minister. Such an act she must consider as failing in sincerity towards the Crown, and justly to be visited by the exercise of her constitutional right of dismissing that Minister. She expects to be kept informed of what passes

*Lajos Kossuth, (1802–1894), Hungarian nationalist leader, who led the short-lived revolt against Austrian rule in 1848–1849.

THERE'S ALWAYS SOMETHING.

"I'M VERY SORRY, PALMERSTON, THAT YOU CANNOT AGREE WITH YOUR FELLOW SERVANTS; BUT AS I DON'T FEEL
INCLINED TO PART WITH JOHN, YOU MUST GO, OF COURSE."

between him and the foreign Ministers before important decisions are taken, based upon that intercourse; to receive the foreign despatches in good time; and to have the drafts for her approval sent to her in sufficient time to make herself acquainted with their contents, before they must be sent off. The Queen thinks it best that Lord John Russell should show this letter to Lord Palmerston.'

His conduct after the *coup d'état*, however, shows clearly how necessary the Queen's letter had been, and how little the Minister had really taken it to heart.

Immediately after the *coup d'état* the Queen and the Prince discussed the line of policy to be observed by England with regard to this event. It was settled that it must be a policy of abstinence and of neutrality. The Queen wrote in this sense to Lord John Russell, who, in a letter, declared his entire agreement. He laid the Queen's letter before the Cabinet, which accepted the line of conduct there pointed out . . .

But at the same time the French ambassador in London, Count Walewski, had informed his Government of a conversation with Lord Palmerston, in which the latter had expressed his 'entire approval' of the *coup d'état* and his 'conviction' that the President could have acted in no other way . . . This led to the Premier, Lord John Russell, demanding a written explanation from Lord Palmerston, who, at the same time, received a message in writing, from the Queen, expressing the same request. Lord Palmerston allowed four days to go by without sending his answer, which naturally could not be satisfactory.

Baron E. von Stockmar, *Memoirs of Baron Stockmar*, ed. F. Max Müller (Longmans, Green, 1872).*

Palmerston Resigns

17 The resignation of Lord Palmerston as a member of the Coalition Ministry under Lord Aberdeen . . . is a masterstroke of that unscrupulous and consummate tactician. Those journals in London which speak for the Ministry carefully inform the public that the event does not grow out of the Eastern difficulty, but that his conscientious lordship, like a

* Baron von Stockmar, (1787–1863), private secretary to Leopold I of Belgium, who in 1837 sent him to England as confidential adviser to Queen Victoria, a role he filled for many years.

true guardian of the British Constitution, quits office because he cannot give his consent to a measure of Parliamentary Reform, even of the pigmy dimensions natural to such a Whig as Lord John Russell . . .* But he has taken good care that the public shall have a different impression, and, in spite of all the declarations of the official organs, it is generally believed that while the Reform Bill is the pretext, the Russian policy of the Cabinet is the real cause . . .

By retiring at such a moment, Lord Palmerston throws off all responsibility from his own shoulders upon those of his late partners. His act becomes a great national event. He is transformed at once into the representative of the people against the Government from which he secedes. He not only saves his own popularity, but he gives the last finish to the unpopularity of his colleagues.

Karl Marx, *The Eastern Question*, eds. E. M. and E. Aveling (London, 1897).

Accused of pro-Russian sympathies

18 The twenty and odd years of tenure of office by Lord Palmerston have, at length, brought forth their fruits. Russia, during this time, assisted by England, has been daily increasing her power,—concentrating her resources,—biding her time. She now sees France a prey to intestine convulsions, and England under the guidance of Lord Aberdeen, who is her declared friend, supported in the Cabinet by Lord Palmerston, who, as Foreign Secretary for upwards of twenty years, has made 'the union of England and Russia' the polar star of all his actions. Russia now believes that the time has arrived for the accomplishment of the will of Peter the Great, and she is about to strike her grand blow for universal empire!

At this important moment unthinking men are heard to shout, 'Palmerston for Premier!' Do they know it was he who held the seals of the Foreign Office when Poland was stolen by an act of 'land piracy' by Russia, while England was the guarantee for the preservation of Poland's nationality?—when Persia was abandoned, and the Affghan War perpetrated?—when the interests of England in Greece were made over to Russia? . . . In short, during all that long period,

---

* Lord John Russell's Reform Bill, which was soon dropped by the Aberdeen coalition government.

while the interests of England and Russia were considered by the British Government to be the same? Do these men reflect upon the consequences that have arisen from the foreign policy of Lord Palmerston, a policy that has mainly contributed to make Russia what she is at the present day? It is to counteract the delusions that are afloat upon this subject that these pages have been written, and to point out that it is not from such a school as this that a Prime Minister is to be chosen for England, at a time when danger is at hand, and Russia is the aggressor.

Anon., *Palmerston for Premier*, The Claims of Lord Palmerston to fill the Post of Prime Minister of England Considered (London, 1854).

Prime Minister at Last

19 The ship of State 'Britannia' had sprung a leak, and was rolling almost without a pilot in the trough of the sea. Men's eyes were opened to the real magnitude of the war, which had been so recklessly begun . . . In the Crimea the gallant armies had won desperate battles, but, so to speak, not a foot of land . . .

An unusually hard winter, and the storms which in an inland sea like the Euxine* are always extremely dangerous, and which wrecked a number of transports, had so weakened the victorious English army, that in the beginning of 1855 only about 10,000 combatants remained, all of whom, partly in the trenches and partly in the camp, now converted into a morass, seemed doomed to perish from hunger, frost, and fever. When the news of these privations and sufferings reached England, and was served up to the public twice a day by the newspapers with exaggerated zeal, a cry of indignation arose, and, as always happens in such cases, the blame was heaped on the men, not the system . . .

When Parliament now assembled on January 23, [1855] the House of Commons showed that they reflected faithfully the feverish excitement of the country. Meanwhile, Lord Aberdeen's position was no enviable one . . . The little, plain-looking but somewhat popular member for Sheffield, Mr. Roebuck**. . . moved for the appointment of a Select Com-

---

* The Black Sea.
** John Arthur Roebuck, (1801–1879), originally a radical who became increasingly reactionary in both his domestic and foreign attitudes.

mittee to inquire into the conduct of the war, in order to ascertain the causes which had reduced the army in the Crimea to such a miserable plight. It is possible that this motion, if not actually inspired by Lord Palmerston, had received his approval . . . That debate ended on the night of January 29 by the motion being carried . . . There was a majority of 157 against the Ministers . . .

As the Tories had voted for Roebuck's motion, and formed the most compact and numerous party of the Opposition, the Queen immediately sent for their leader, Lord Derby. The Earl declined to undertake the responsibility of forming an effective Cabinet at such a critical moment, unless Lord Palmerston and the Peelites would consent to serve with him, and left it with the Queen to attempt other combinations, promising, however, in the event of those attempts failing, to place his services at her Majesty's disposal. The Queen now sent for Lord John Russell. Self-sufficient as ever, he undertook the task, but he reaped what he had sown, and was forced in a few days to confess his inability to undertake the Government. Finally the Queen turned to Lord Palmerston. This was a hard resolve to make, but it was a necessity. Palmerston not only had the ear of the House and the favour of the people, but, what was now almost more important than either, the full confidence of Napoleon, without whose assistance it was hopeless to think of bringing the war to an honourable termination. Prince Albert, who knew the noble Lord pretty well, and who said to me once afterwards, 'I cannot respect that man, for he always prefers his own interests to those of the nation,' was too good a patriot not to see that Palmerston had become the man of the hour. Moreover, there was no disguising the fact that events had to some extent justified Lord Palmerston, and that his over-hasty recognition of the *coup d'état* had rendered possible that alliance which was more necessary now than ever.

Count Vitzthum, *St. Petersburg and London in the years 1852–1864*, ed. Henry Reeve (Longmans, Green, 1887).

Physical courage

20 The death of Lord Palmerston is still so recent an event, and his public character has been so amply eulogised, that I should not have touched upon his name, had I not been able to add

one or two traits less generally known, characteristic of this remarkable man. One of these, of which I had frequent professional knowledge, was his wonderful power of *mastering*, I might call it *ignoring*, bodily pain. I have seen him, under a fit of gout which would have sent other men groaning to their couches, continue his work of writing or reading on public business almost without abatement, amidst the chaos of papers which covered the floor as well as the tables of his room. As a patient he was never fretful, but obedient in every way except as to this very point. And here, indeed, though I at first remonstrated against these unusual labours during illness, I soon learnt that such remonstrance was not only fruitless but injudicious. To Lord Palmerston work was itself a remedy.

Sir Henry Holland, *Recollections of Past Life* (Longmans, Green, 1872).*

Final Days

21 Those around him could not fail to feel anxiety about his evident state of weakness, not only for the moment, but at the prospect of his again meeting Parliament as Prime Minister. That he himself felt the same anxiety for the future was clear; and one morning, about a fortnight before he died, I witnessed an incident which was both evidence of this and also very characteristic of the man. There were some high railings immediately opposite the front door, and Lord Palmerston, coming out of the house without his hat, went straight up to them, after casting a look all round to see that no one was looking, He then climbed deliberately over the top rail down to the ground on the other side, turned round, climbed back again, and then went indoors. It was clear that he had come out to test his strength, and to find out for himself in a practical way how far he was gaining or losing ground. Not that he had any excessive dread of death, for, as he put it one day, in homely fashion, to his doctor, when pressing for a frank opinion as to his state, 'When a man's time is up there is no use in repining.'. . .

A chill caught while out driving brought on inflammation of the kidneys, and on October 18, 1865, within two days of completing his eighty-first year, he closed his earthly career. The

*Sir Henry Holland, (1788–1873), appointed physician in ordinary to Queen Victoria, 1852.

half-opened cabinet-box on his table, and the unfinished letter on his desk, testified that he was at his post to the last.

Evelyn Ashley, *The Life and Correspondence of Henry John Temple*, 'Viscount Palmerston' (London, 1879).*

The Truest Englishman

22 One of the most popular statesmen, one of the kindliest gentlemen, and one of the truest Englishmen that ever filled the office of Premier, is today lost to the country. The news of Lord Palmerston's death will be received in every home throughout these islands, from the palace to the cottage, with a feeling like that of personal bereavement . . . The secret and source of his great popularity was his boundless sympathy with all classes of his countrymen . . . Nor was this kindness and affability merely superficial. It may not be generally known, that when an attempt was made on his life by a crazy officer at the War Office, his first act was to draw a check for the expenses of his assailant's defence. That act was characteristic of the man; and Englishmen were proud of him, not so much because he bearded foreign despots in his prime, or exhibited marvellous physical activity in his old age, as because they believed him to be a stout-hearted and benevolent statesman of the good old English stock . . .

He has left none like him—none who can rally round him so many followers of various opinions, none who can give us so happy a respite from the violence of party-warfare, none who can bring to the work of statesmanship so precious a store of recollections. It is impossible not to feel that Lord Palmerston's death marks an epoch in English politics . . . Other Ministers may carry into successful effect organic reforms from which he shrunk. Others may introduce a new spirit into our foreign relations, and abandon the secret diplomacy which he never failed to support. Others may advise Her Majesty with equal sagacity, and sway the House of Commons with equal or greater eloquence; but his place in the hearts of the people will not be filled so easily. The name of Lord Palmerston, once the terror of the Continent, will long be connected in the minds of Englishmen with an epoch of unbroken peace and unparalleled prosperity . . .

The Times, October 19, 1865.

* Evelyn Ashley, (1836–1907), son of the seventh Earl of Shaftesbury, author and Liberal M.P., private secretary to Palmerston from 1858 to 1865.

The Great Flaw in his Character

23 Lord Palmerston is certainly one of, if not quite the ablest of the statesmen I have ever met with in all my official career. He possesses all the aptitude and capacity which most contributes to form such a man in England—extensive and varied information, indefatigable activity, an iron constitution, inexhaustible mental resources and great facility of speech in Parliament. Without being what is called a great *debater,* his style of eloquence is biting and satirical, his talent lying more in his power of crushing an adversary under the weight of his irony and sarcasm, than of convincing his auditors; and furthermore, he has great social qualities and highly finished manners.

There is one point in his character, however, which to my mind, entirely outweighs all these advantages, and would prevent his being considered in the light of a real statesman—he allows his passions to influence him in public affairs, to the extent of sometimes sacrificing the greatest interests to his personal feelings. It may be said, that nearly every political question resolves itself with him into a personal one; and whilst seeming to defend the interests of his country, it is nearly always those of his hatred or revenge that he is serving. He is very skilful in hiding this secret motive, under what I might call, patriotic appearances; and it is by this same skill that he nearly always contrives to influence a considerable portion of public opinion, which he leads in whatever direction his own personal passions indicate. . . . There are few Englishmen who know as well as he does, how to excite John Bull's patriotic feelings.

Memoirs of the Prince de Talleyrand, ed. Duc de Broglie (London, 1891).*

Not a Warmonger

24 No view of Lord Palmerston will less stand the test of examination than that which generally prevailed of him about twenty years ago, as a rash, hot-headed impetuous Foreign Secretary. We do not say that interference with foreign nations was not part of his theory of foreign policy, and at one time a much

---

* Charles Maurice de Talleyrand, (1754–1838), French statesman, who negotiated with Palmerston over the establishment of an independent Belgium, while he was ambassador in London from 1830 to 1834.

more important part of his theory than in recent years. But there has never been a time when he had not a head cool enough to weigh cautiously even his own favourite political projects, and to sacrifice them decisively where he saw them to be impracticable . . .

Lord Palmerston's unwillingness to act without clear hope of success was really a more conspicuous feature of his foreign policy than the two or three great *coups* by which he is remembered. His greatest single achievement—the one brilliant stroke of which he was himself probably most proud —was the triple defeat of Russia, France, and Mehemet Ali, in 1840. Yet this happy stroke did but retrieve a series of failures in our Eastern policy in which . . . Lord Palmerston had acquiesced because he knew that he had no adequate resources for success. Indeed, looking to Lord Palmerston's views and traditionary principles, the remarkable feature about his policy is rather the number of cases in which he *refrained* from attempting what he wished, from motives of caution, than the number of cases in which he did anything hazardous for what he deemed a great end. He accepted many humiliations from Russia, some severe humiliations from France, at least one grave humiliation from Spain, and one even from Naples, rather than risk war.

Richard Holt Hutton, 'The Pall Mall Gazette, October, 1865', reprinted in *Studies in Parliament* (Longmans, Green, 1866).*

A LATER ASSESSMENT

No Fixed Principles

25 Lord Palmerston's creed was never the creed of the far-seeing philosopher; it was the creed of a sensible and sagacious but still commonplace man. . . . He had a great difficulty as a Foreign Minister. He had no real conception of any mode of life except that with which he was familiar. His idea, his fixed idea, was that the Turks were a highly improving and civilised race, and it was impossible to beat into him their essentially barbaric and unindustrial character . . . A man of the world is not an imaginative animal, and Lord Palmerston was by incur-

* Richard Holt Hutton, (1826–1897), Unitarian minister, and journalist, appointed editor of the *Spectator* in 1861.

able nature a man of the world . . . Even the best part of his foreign policy was alloyed with this defect. The mantle of Canning had descended on him, and the creed and interests of Canning. He was most eager to use the strong influence of England to support free institutions—to aid 'the Liberal party' was the phrase in those days everywhere on the Continent. And no aim could be juster and better—it was the best way in which English strength could be used. But he failed in the instructed imagination and delicate perception necessary to its best attainment . . . According to the notions of the present age, too, foreign policy should be regulated by abstract, or at least, comprehensive principles, but Lord Palmerston had no such principles. He prided himself on his exploits in Europe, but it is by his instincts in England that he will be remembered.

Walter Bagehot, *Biographical Studies* (Longmans, Green, 1881).*

MODERN VIEWS

Love of Power

26 Palmerston's greatness lies not so much in himself, or in his policy, as in the age which he represented . . . Palmerston was lucky because his diplomatic currency had a sounder basis than that of any of his rivals; and so formidable was Britain in his day that it would have been a bad foreign minister indeed who would not have achieved some notable successes. It was not Palmerston who was great, but Britain; and Britain has never been greater, before or since. Sometimes he used it for unworthy objects, or made mountains out of molehills, from love of demonstrating Britain's strength. Sometimes he used it to succour oppressed peoples, hunted refugees, or tortured slaves. To Palmerston the sense of power was always more important than the purpose for which that power was being exercised: and contemporaries and posterity, in praising Palmerston, have praised him not for himself but for his incarnation of Britain at her peak of glory.

Gavin Burns Henderson, *Crimean War Diplomacy and Other Historical Essays* (Jackson, Son & Co., Glasgow, 1947).

* Walter Bagehot, (1826–1877), political commentator, who wrote a classic work on *The English Constitution*.

Policy of Compromise

27 No man controls the foreign policy of a country for nearly
thirty years and lives to see himself a parliamentary dictator—
dictator too in a parliament that contained Gladstone, John
Russell, Bright, Cobden and Disraeli—merely because he has
a ready wit and a thick skin; Palmerston was the hero of
England because he deserved to be. As a European statesman,
his objects, though he would have hated to confess it, were
the same as Metternich's—the preservation of Peace and
Order; but he did not confuse peace with petrification or order
with death . . . But he differed violently and fundamentally as
to the means by which Peace and Order were to be preserved.
His method was the method of compromise—to grant popular
demands while they were moderate and tentative, so as not to
be compelled to grant much more extreme demands later . . .
   Palmerston's encouragement of reform is often represented
as mere meddlesomeness, from which British interests could
gain nothing. But this is very far from the truth; the British
middle-classes supported Palmerston so steadfastly, just
because all his policy was conducted for their benefit. At a
time when England was becoming the workshop of the world
and when English merchants were to be found in every country
in Europe, it was obviously to the interest of England that the
course of trade should not be interrupted by revolution or war,
and this preservation of the peace of Europe, both domestic
and international, was the primary object of Palmerston's
policy . . . Therefore, when he saw the Continental statesmen
doing everything in their power, as he believed, to make
revolution inevitable, he set out, not very tactfully, to stop
them and to encourage those moderate reforms in which he
saw the only guarantee against revolution.
   A. J. P. Taylor, *The Italian Problem in European Diplomacy,
1847–1849* (Manchester University Press, 1934).

Relations with the Press

28 In Lord Palmerston's hands, therefore, the voter felt confident
that his pride, his interest, and his conscience were all in safe
keeping. He was in a peculiar manner a representative man—
'Minister for England' . . . He belonged to a political party,
but it was his object to transcend party issues. His appeal was,

in the strict sense of the word, a democratic one. He never missed an opportunity of appearing to advantage in a daily paper. Every political group employed some newspaper to represent its point of view, and even, on occasion, to make official statements on its behalf, but Palmerston was probably the first British statesman who deliberately ingratiated himself with papers of all shades of opinion. After his death, the editor of a prominent paper wrote: 'There was never a man who was so great a favourite personally, not with the reporters only, but with all the gentlemen filling the higher positions on the Press, as the late Lord Palmerston . . . It often happened during the prolonged Premiership or Foreign Secretaryship of Lord Palmerston, that on representing to him both in Hants or at Tiverton* that if the time fixed for his speech could not be altered, the reporters from London would not be able to reach their respective offices with their report until too late, he would immediately apply to alter the programmes so that the reporters should not be disappointed.' And, on occasions when an alteration of the programme would not serve, he was willing to make private orations in his room at the hotel, which the reporters could convey punctually for the morning's paper.

It was this personal appeal to the public which differentiated Lord Palmerston from other statesmen of his period and which so often infuriated them . . . His actions as Foreign Minister were his own, not those of his Government, and when he spoke in Parliament he was not so much concerned with the faces he saw round him as with the greater public which would read his speech in the newspaper the next morning.

Kingsley Martin, *The Triumph of Lord Palmerston* (Hutchinson, 1963).

29 For thirty-seven years Palmerston was immersed in the study of foreign affairs, and for nearly twenty-four of them in the conduct of foreign affairs, as Foreign Secretary or Prime Minister. He was intimately involved in them longer than any modern statesman . . . But they do Palmerston and his public wrong who think he owed his popularity entirely to mere 'jingoism' of a brash and shallow kind. . . .

Palmerston did not wish to wage wars, though he despised

* His constituencies.

diplomats who shrank from using every card in the pack, including the threat (or more often the hint) of war. In large crises he was grave and careful, if sanguine and intrepid, and it is likely that, if he had controlled policy in 1853, Britain would have avoided the one considerable war in which she was involved in his time . . . Palmerston did not have to play the part of John Bull; he lived it. Except in the great crises of relations with France or Russia, he refused to be deterred from saying what he felt simply because he happened to be Foreign Secretary or prime minister. He dared to use the authority of great offices of state to add weight to his convictions. And those convictions were congenial to the Britain of the 1850s.

Donald Southgate, *The Most English Minister* (Macmillan, 1966).

3. Benjamin Disraeli, Earl of Beaconsfield, 1804-1881

There has never been a prime minister quite like Benjamin Disraeli—the novelist, wit and man-about-town of Jewish ancestry. He was unique. But was he a mere adventurer, or did he contribute something of lasting value to the Conservative party? That question was passionately debated in his lifetime and continues to this day.

By the time he was twenty-two, Disraeli had already achieved a certain notoriety in society through the publication of his novel, *Vivian Grey*, in 1826 (1). But he also had political ambitions and an individual political philosophy based upon the ideas of 'one nation' and the necessity for moderate reform (6–10). He stood for Parliament three times before he was elected an M.P. for Maidstone in 1837 (11–12). His maiden speech was a fiasco, though according to at least one observer it attracted the favourable attention of Sir Robert Peel (13–14).

From an early age, Disraeli determined to marry for money, of which he was in constant need through the extravagance of his tastes (15). In 1839, he married a rich widow, which produced some anti-semitic sneers (16). But the marriage proved to be happy and satisfactory to them both.

In 1841, Disraeli was bitterly disappointed when Peel failed to offer him a post in his ministry. He resumed his writing and published two of his best-known novels, *Coningsby* in 1844 and *Sybil, or the Two Nations,* in the following year (17). In 1846, he seized the chance to make a biting denunciation of Peel's proposal to repeal the Corn Laws.* His brilliant, witty speech made him the hero of the squires and landed gentry in the Conservative party (18).

Within three years he became leader of the party in the Commons. In 1852 he held office for the first time—as Chancellor of the Exchequer in Derby's short-lived administration (19). He held the same post again from 1858–1859. But

* See pp. 20–1.

his position in the party was by no means secure. In 1860 the orthodox, Conservative *Quarterly Review* published an attack on him, though the *Times* came to his defence (20–21). In 1866, Disraeli became Chancellor of the Exchequer for the third time, and as leader of the Commons showed great skill in steering the Second Reform Bill, designed 'to dish the Whigs', through the House (22). In February, 1868, Lord Derby resigned as prime minister for health reasons, and Disraeli was appointed his successor. But the Conservatives were defeated in the general election that autumn.

In 1874 Disraeli became prime minister for the second time. His government carried out a number of important reforms concerning trade unions, housing, and public health, but Disraeli's main interests were in foreign affairs—and the Empire. In 1875 he was personally responsible for buying the shares in the Suez Canal company, which had been held by the Khedive of Egypt (23–24). In the following year he succeeded in passing a Bill which made Queen Victoria Empress of India —much to her delight (25). In the same year he was created Earl of Beaconsfield.

His greatest triumph in foreign policy came at the Congress of Berlin, called to settle the Eastern Question. When the Bulgarian revolt against Turkish rule was suppressed with great brutality, liberal opinion in Britain was shocked. Gladstone denounced the Turks in his pamphlet, *The Bulgarian Horrors and the Question of the East,* published in 1876.* In the following year, Russia declared war on Turkey. The British were so alarmed by Russian successes that a wave of jingoistic feeling swept through the country (26). The war between Russia and Turkey was ended by the Treaty of San Stefano, 1878. Under this treaty the size of the Turkish empire was greatly reduced by creating a large autonomous state of Bulgaria. Disraeli was opposed to this weakening of Turkey— the traditional bulwark against Russian expansionism—and succeeded in having the treaty modified at the Congress of Berlin, 1878. Disraeli and Lord Salisbury, the Foreign Secretary, were welcomed home as heroes—for achieving 'peace with honour' (27–29). Under the agreement, Britain gained the right to occupy Cyprus, though even some contemporary school books expressed doubts about the wisdom of the move (30).

* See pp. 122–4.

At the general election in 1880, the Conservatives were defeated. Disraeli died in the following year and was buried at Hughenden. Queen Victoria, who was a great admirer of Disraeli, was prevented by protocol from attending the funeral: she paid a private visit to the vault four days later (31) One conspicuous absentee from the funeral was Gladstone, who paid a parliamentary tribute to his old enemy and rival, though in his heart he still detested him (32–33).

Criticism of Disraeli—which often had an anti-semitic tinge —did not end with his death. J. A. Froude thought his achievements were negligible, while the Earl of Cromer saw him as a semi-Oriental, self-seeking opportunist (34–35). There were others, however, who praised him for making Conservatives adjust to the changed times (36).

In modern times, there is still a wide spectrum of opinion, ranging from those who believe that he was a true English patriot who had a lasting impact on his party, to others who think that he retarded the development of Conservatism by twenty years (37–41). For some of his individual achievements, such as the Treaty of Berlin, there is now much less general regard (42). As a writer, particularly of letters, he still merits serious attention, though opinions about the quality of his novels remain divided (43).

Further Reading

Robert Blake, *Disraeli* (Eyre and Spottiswoode, 1966). (There is also a shorter biography by the same author in the *Clarendon Biographies,* Oxford University Press, 1969).
B. R. Jerman, *The Young Disraeli* (Princeton, 1960).
Paul Smith, *Disraelian Conservatism and Social Reform* (Routledge and Kegan Paul, 1967).

CHARACTER AND APPEARANCE

The Young Dandy

1 When he was very young and had made his first appearance in London society as the author of *Vivian Grey,* there was something almost incredible in his aspect. She* assured me that she

* Helen Selina Sheridan, Lady Dufferin, (1807–1867), one of the three beautiful granddaughters of the playwright. In his later years, Disraeli confessed that she had been 'his chief admiration'.

did not exaggerate in the slightest degree in describing to me his dress when she first met him at a dinner party. He wore a black velvet coat lined with satin, purple trousers with a gold band running down the outside seam, a scarlet waistcoat, long lace ruffles falling down to the tips of his fingers, white gloves with several brilliant rings outside them, and long black ringlets rippling down upon his shoulders. It seemed impossible that such a Guy Fawkes could have been tolerated in any society. His audacity, which has proved more perennial than brass, was always the solid foundation of his character. She told him, however, that he made a fool of himself by appearing in such fantastic shape, and he afterwards modified his costume, but he was never to be put down.

The Correspondence of John Lothrop Motley, ed. George William Curtis (John Murray, 1889).*

A Moody, Lonely Man

2 Lord Beaconsfield in society was capricious of mood. He sometimes sparkled with epigram and paradox, and sometimes fell into a fit of brooding silence. His hosts and hostesses could not count on him. He might delight the dinner-table with his talk, or he might sit mute, with his head bent over his plate. He was not very companionable even with his colleagues on the Treasury Bench, or on the front bench of the Opposition. He had his chosen friends, to whom he was always kind and confiding, but his colleagues in general, like his hosts and hostesses, could not always count upon his mood . . . For all the splendour of his opportunities and his successes he was a lonely, self-sufficing man.

Justin McCarthy, M.P., *A History of Our Own Times from 1880 to the Diamond Jubilee* (Chatto & Windus, 1897).

Concern for Tenants

3 His great sympathy with his tenants was beyond all praise . . . He was in the habit constantly of visiting his tenants, sitting down and chatting with them on rural matters; inquiring into the sanitary arrangements of their homes; and, by his sympathetic interest in all connected with them, winning their

* John Lothrop Motley, (1814–1877), American author of the well-known, but superseded, *The Rise of the Dutch Republic.*

hearts and securing their confidence. One tenant in particular, who was suffering from rheumatism, inhabited a large farmhouse which, like many in the neighbourhood, had floors of brick. Laughingly referring to this as the probable cause of his malady, the Earl took up the matter seriously, and the next day sent a workman to remove the brick floor and substitute a wooden one . . .

One or two anecdotes will suffice to show the real simplicity of mind of this great master of sarcastic repartee. One morning a labourer at Hughenden,* addressing his lordship's coachman, and not knowing that his lordship was in the carriage, inquired, 'How's the old man today?' 'I am quite well, thank you,' replied the Earl, looking suddenly out of the carriage window, and, no doubt, thoroughly enjoying the joke. On another occasion, he was overtaken in his own grounds by two intrusive women, who, not knowing him, asked, 'Is this Dizzy's place?' The Earl courteously replied, 'It is'; and directed them to a part of the grounds where they could obtain a good view of the house. The women were somewhat confused when they afterwards found they had been addressing the owner.

Henry Lake, *Personal Reminiscences of the Right Hon. Benjamin Disraeli, Earl of Beaconsfield* (Cassell & Co., n.d.).

His Great Kindness

4 Those who did not know Lord Beaconsfield intimately can scarcely realise the depth of kindness, almost tenderness, in his nature, showing itself silently, but ceaselessly, to all around him . . . While walking by the side of the little stream with the writer, a poor old man came up to him. Lord Beaconsfield spoke in a particularly kind manner to him, and listened to his story. The poor old man rambled in his talk about a dead bird he had found and held in his hand. Lord Beaconsfield heard him patiently, but after looking at the bird, said, 'It pains me to see it; take it away.' He afterwards explained that the old man was what the Scotch called 'daft', but harmless; that he had long employed him at Hughenden, and had provided for his comfort, and liked him to roam in the park.

Janetta Manners, *Some Personal Recollections of the Later*

---

* Hughenden Manor, just north of High Wycombe, which Disraeli bought with borrowed money, in 1848. It is now a Disraeli Museum.

Years of the Earl of Beaconsfield (William Blackwood, 1881).*

A Strange and Impressive Figure

5 It was, indeed, a strange and impressive figure that you might meet, any day, in the late seventies during the session, sauntering slowly on Corry's** arm down Whitehall. A frame, once large and powerful, now shrunken and obviously in physical decay, but preserving a conscious dignity, and, whenever aware of observation, regaining with effort an erect attitude; a countenance of extreme pallor set rigidly like a mask; a high, broad forehead, and straight, well-formed nose; eyes deeply sunken and usually lustreless, but capable of sudden brightening in moments of excitement; a wide, flexible mouth, and firm chin; the whole face in a setting of still abundant hair, kept perennially as black as coal, and arranged with a remnant of curliness over the ears, with one conspicuous curl in the centre of the forehead, and with a small tuft under the chin . . . The curl on the forehead, which came naturally in youth, was a work of careful art in age. 'It was kept in place,' writes one who, when young, was admitted to the great man's intimacy, 'by being damped and then a yellow bandanna tied tightly round it in front, with the ends down his back, till it was dry. I have thus seen him in his bedroom, attired in addition in a dressing-gown of many colours and a silk cord round his waist.'

W. F. Monypenny and G. E. Buckle, *The Life of Benjamin Disraeli Earl of Beaconsfield* (John Murray, 1929).

CONTEMPORARY VIEWS

Disraeli's Philosophy

6 The Whig party has ever been odious to the English people . . . The Whigs are an anti-national party. In order to accomplish their object of establishing an oligarchical republic, and of concentrating the government of the state in the hands of a few great families, the Whigs are compelled to declare war against

---

* Janetta Manners, Duchess of Rutland, wife of seventh Duke of Rutland, who as Lord John Manners was a fellow member with Disraeli of the 'Young England' movement in the 1840s.

** Montagu Corry, later Lord Rowton, his private secretary.

all those great national institutions, the power and influence of which, present obstacles to the fulfilment of their purpose. It is these institutions which make us a nation. Without our Crown, our Church, our Universities, our great municipal and commercial Corporations [and] our Magistracy . . . the inhabitants of England, instead of being a nation, would present only a mass of individuals . . . The Tory party in the country is the national party; it is the really democratic party of England.

Disraeli the Younger, *Vindication of the English Constitution in a Letter to a Noble and Learned Lord* (London, 1835).*

7 The basis of English society is Equality. But here let us distinguish: there are two kinds of equality; there is the equality that levels and destroys, and the equality that elevates and creates . . . Thus the meanest subject of our King is born to great and important privileges; an Englishman, however humble may be his birth, whether he be doomed to the plough or destined to the loom, is born to the noblest of all inheritances; . . . he is born to freedom, he is born to justice, and he is born to property. There is no station to which he may not aspire; there is no master whom he is obliged to serve; there is no magistrate who dares imprison him against the law . . Thus the English in politics are as the old Hebrews in religion, 'a favoured and peculiar people'. . . .
Ibid.

8 A Tory, and a Radical, I understand; a Whig, a democratic aristocrat, I cannot comprehend. If the Tories indeed despair of restoring the aristocratic principle, and are sincere in their avowal that the State cannot be governed with the present machinery, it is their duty to coalesce with the Radicals, and permit both political nick-names to merge in the common, the intelligible, and dignified title of a National Party.

B. Disraeli, *What is He?* (London, 1833).

9 Gentlemen, the programme of the Conservative party is to maintain the Constitution of the country . . . When the banner of Republicanism is unfurled, when the fundamental

*In some of his early writings, Disraeli called himself 'Disraeli the Younger' to distinguish himself from his father Isaac D'Israeli, (1766–1848), a miscellaneous writer, best-known for his *Curiosities of Literature*.

principles of our institutions are controverted, I think perhaps it may not be inconvenient that I should make some few practical remarks upon the character of our Constitution— upon that monarchy, limited by the co-ordinate authority of estates of the realm, which, under the title of Queen, Lords, and Commons, has contributed so greatly to the prosperity of this country, and with the maintenance of which I believe that prosperity is bound up. Gentlemen, since the settlement of that Constitution, now nearly two centuries ago, England has never experienced a revolution, though there is no country in which there had been so continuous and such considerable change. How is this? Because the wisdom of your forefathers placed the prize of supreme power without the sphere of human passions. Whatever the struggle of parties, whatever the strife of factions, whatever the excitement and exaltation of the public mind, there has always been something in this country round which all classes and all parties could rally, representing the majesty of law, the administration of justice, and being at the same time the security for every man's rights and the fountain of honour. . . .

I know it will be said, gentlemen, that, however beautiful in theory, the personal influence of the Sovereign is now absorbed in the responsibility of the Minister. I think you will find there is some fallacy in this view. The principles of the English Constitution do not contemplate the absence of personal influence on the part of the Sovereign; and, if they did, the principles of human nature would prevent the fulfil- ment of such a theory . . . From the earliest moment of his accession that Sovereign is placed in constant communication with the most able statesmen of the period, and of all parties... The longer the reign, the influence of that Sovereign must proportionately increase . . .

Gentlemen, the influence of the Crown is not confined merely to political affairs. England is a domestic country. Here the home is revered and the hearth is sacred. The nation is represented by a family—the Royal Family; and if that family is educated with a sense of responsibility and a sentiment of public duty, it is difficult to exaggerate the salutary influence it may exercise over a nation. It is not merely the influence upon manners; it is not merely that it may be a model for refinement and for good taste—it affects the heart as well as the intelligence of the people; and in the hour of public adversity

... the nation rallies round the Family and the Throne ...

It is not merely the authority of the Throne that is now disputed, but the character and influence of the House of Lords are held up by some to public disregard ... What, gentlemen, is the first quality which is required in a Second Chamber? Without doubt, independence. What is the best foundation of independence? Without doubt, property. The Prime Minister of England has only recently told us, and I believe he spoke quite accurately, that the average income of the members of the House of Lords is £20,000 per annum ... It is, generally speaking, territorial property; and one of the elements of territorial property is that it is representative. Now, for illustration, suppose—which God forbid—there was no House of Commons, and some Englishman—I will take him from either end of the island—a Cumberland or a Cornish man, finds himself aggrieved. The Cumbrian says, 'This conduct I experience is most unjust. I know a Cumberland man in the House of Lords, the Earl of Carlisle or the Earl of Lonsdale; I will go to him; he will never see a Cumberland man ill-treated.' The Cornish man will say: 'I will go to the Lord of Port Eliot; his family have sacrificed themselves before this for the liberties of Englishmen, and he will get justice done me'. . .

The House of Commons represents the constituency* of England, and I am here to show that no addition to the elements of that constituency has placed the House of Commons in a different relation to the Throne and the House of Lords from that it has always constitutionally occupied ... Gentlemen, it appears by the census that the population at this time is about 32,000,000. It is shown by the last registration that ... the constituency of the United Kingdom may be placed at 2,300,000. So, gentlemen, it at once appears that there are nearly 30,000,000 people in this country who are as much represented by the House of Lords as by the House of Commons, and who, for the protection of their rights, must mainly depend upon the majesty of the Throne . . .

Lord Grey, in his measure of 1832 ... accorded to the middle classes great and salutary franchises; but he not only made no provision for the representation of the working classes in the Constitution, but he absolutely abolished those

* The electorate.

(ancient franchises* which the working classes had enjoyed and exercised from time immemorial. That was the origin of Chartism, and of that electoral uneasiness which existed in this country more or less for thirty years . . . When Lord Derby became Prime Minister, affairs had arrived at such a point that it was of the first moment that the question should be sincerely dealt with. He had to encounter great difficulties, but he accomplished his purpose with the support of a united party**. . . .

In attempting to legislate upon social matters, the great object is to be practical. I think public attention as regards these matters ought to be concentrated upon sanitary legislation. That is a wide subject, and, if properly treated, comprises almost every consideration which has a just claim upon legislative interference. Pure air, pure water, the inspection of unhealthy habitations, the adulteration of food, these and many kindred matters may be legitimately dealt with by the Legislature . . . Gentlemen, it is impossible to overrate the importance of the subject. After all, the first consideration of a Minister should be the health of the people.

Speech at the Free Trade Hall, Manchester, April 3, 1872 (London, n.d.).

10 If you look to the history of this country since the advent of Liberalism—40 years ago—you will find that there has been no effort so continuous, so subtle, supported by so much energy, and carried on with so much ability and acumen, as the attempts of Liberalism to effect the disintegration of the Empire of England. And, gentlemen, of all its efforts, this is the one which has been the nearest to success . . . It has been proved to all of us that we have lost money by our colonies. It has been shewn with precise, with mathematical demonstration, that there never was a jewel in the Crown of England that was so truly costly as the possession of India . . .

Well, what has been the result of this attempt during the reign of Liberalism for the disintegration of the Empire? It has entirely failed. But how has it failed? Through the sympathy of the Colonies with the Mother Country. They have decided that the Empire shall not be destroyed, and in my opinion no Minister in this country will do his duty who

---

* e.g. potwallopers (heads of households which had separate fireplaces) and scot and lot voters (ratepayers) in boroughs. After 1832 these electors were allowed to vote for the rest of their lives.

** i.e. the passing of the Second Reform Bill, 1867.

neglects any opportunity of reconstructing as much as possible of our Colonial Empire, and of responding to those distant sympathies which may become the source of incalculable strength and happiness to this land. . . . The views which I expressed in the great capital of the county of Lancaster have been held up to derision by the Liberal Press. A leading member—a very rising member, at least, among the new Liberal members— denounced them the other day as the 'policy of sewage'. Well, it may be the 'policy of sewage' to a Liberal member of Parliament. But to one of the labouring multitude of England, who has found fever always to be one of the inmates of his household—who has, year after year, seen stricken down the children of his loins, on whose sympathy and material support he has looked with hope and confidence, it is not a 'policy of sewage', but a question of life and death.
    Speech of the Right Hon. B. Disraeli M.P. at the Crystal Palace, on Monday, June 24, 1872 (London, n.d.).

Political Ambitions

11 *February 7, 1833*
Went to the House of Commons afterwards to hear Bulwer adjourn the House; was there yesterday during the whole debate—one of the finest we have had for years. Bulwer spoke, but he is physically disqualified for an orator, and, in spite of all his exertions, never can succeed . . . Heard Macaulay's best speech, Sheil and Charles Grant. Macaulay admirable; but, between ourselves, I could floor them all. This *entre nous*: I was never more confident of anything than that I could carry everything before me in that House. The time will come . . .

April 28, 1835
I have just left the hustings, and have gained the show of hands, which no blue* candidate ever did before. This, though an idle ceremony in most places, is of great account here, for the potwallopers** of Taunton are as eloquent as those of Athens, and we gain votes by such a demonstration . . .

* i.e. Conservative. Blue was then, and still is, the party colour.
** Electors whose qualification for voting was being the head of a household. The only qualification was to have a separate fireplace at which to cook their food, so many of the working classes qualified. This franchise was abolished by the Act of 1832, but the existing potwallopers were allowed, under certain conditions, to continue voting for the rest of their lives.

THE RISING GENERATION—IN PARLIAMENT.

Peel. "WELL, MY LITTLE MAN, WHAT ARE YOU GOING TO DO THIS SESSION, EH?"
D——li (the Juvenile). "WHY—AW—AW—I'VE MADE ARRANGEMENTS—AW—TO SMASH—AW—EVERYBODY."

Punch, January 30, 1847

Wednesday night: April 30, 1835
There is no place like *Taunton,* not that I can win this time;...
but come in at the general election I must, for I have promises
of two-thirds of the electors. I live in a rage of enthusiasm;
even my opponents promise to vote for me *next time.* The
fatigue is awful. Two long speeches today and nine hours'
canvass on foot in a blaze of repartee. I am quite exhausted
and can scarcely see to write.
*Lord Beaconsfield's Correspondence with his Sister, 1832–
1852,* ed. Ralph Disraeli (John Murray, 1886).

Elected M.P. for Maidstone

November 15, 1837
12 I took my seat this morning. I went down to the House with
Wyndham Lewis* at two o'clock, and found it very full, the
members standing in groups and chatting. About three o'clock
there was a cry of 'Order! Order!' all took their seats (myself
on the second bench, behind Sir Robert Peel) . . . Then
Abercromby,** who looked like an old laundress, mumbled
and moaned some dulness, and was then carried to the chair,
and said a little more, amid a faint cheer. To me of course
the scene was exciting enough, but none could share my
feelings, except new members. Peel was a great deal at the
Carlton*** yesterday. He welcomed me very warmly, and all
noticed his cordial demeanour. He looks very well, and asked
me to join a small dinner at the Carlton on Thursday . . .

November 21, 1837
Yesterday, after being obliged to go down to the House at
eleven, to ensure a house for members to swear, I went to a
great meeting at Peel's. There must have been 300 members.
Peel addressed, full of spirit, and apparently eager for action.
Thence again to the House, where we were summoned to the
Lords at two o'clock. The rush was terrific; Abercromby himself nearly thrown down and trampled upon, and his mace-
bearer banging the members' heads with his gorgeous weapon,
and cracking skulls with impunity. I was fortunate enough to

* The other M.P. for Maidstone. Just over a year after Wyndham Lewis died in
March, 1838, Disraeli married his rich widow.
** James Abercromby, later Lord Dunfermline (1776–1858), Speaker of the House
of Commons from 1835 to 1839.
*** The Conservative club founded by the Duke of Wellington in 1832.

escape, however, and also to ensure an entry. It was a magnificent spectacle. The Queen looked admirably, no feathers but a diamond tiara . . .

From the Lords I escaped, almost at the hazard of our lives, with Mahon, who is now most cordial, and we at length succeeded in gaining the Carlton, having several times been obliged to call upon the police and Military to protect us as we attempted to break the line, but the moment the magical words 'Member of Parliament' were uttered all the authorities came to our assistance, all gave way, and we passed everywhere. You never saw two such figures, our hats crushed and covered with mud, and the mobocracy envying us our privileges, calling out 'Jim Crow'* as we stalked through the envious files.

I went down, after refitting at the Carlton, for about half an hour, during which I tried to scribble to you. The seat I succeeded in securing behind Peel I intend if possible to appropriate to myself . . . I then left the House at ten o'clock, none of us having dined. The tumult and excitement great. I dined, or rather supped, at the Carlton with a large party off oysters, Guinness, and broiled bones, and got to bed at half-past twelve o'clock. Thus ended the most remarkable day hitherto of my life.

Ibid.

Maiden Speech

13 Nothing was so easy as to laugh. He wished before he sat down to show the House clearly their position . . . He would certainly gladly hear a cheer even though it came from the lips of a political opponent. He was not at all surprised at the reception which he had experienced. He had begun several times many things, and he had often succeeded at last. He would sit down now, but the time would come when they would hear him.

Disraeli, Speech in House of Commons, December 7th, 1837 (Hansard, 1838).

Peel's Encouragement

14 It is particularly deserving of mention that even Sir Robert

---

* 'Jim Crow', a well-known London street-clown, who dressed in rags but pretended to be a member of fashionable society. He died in a workhouse in 1851.

Peel, who very rarely cheers any honourable gentleman, not even the most able and accomplished speakers of his own party greeted Mr. D'Israeli's speech with a prodigality of applause, which must have been severely trying to the worthy baronet's lungs. Mr. D'Israeli spoke from the second row of benches immediately opposite the Speaker's chair. Sir Robert, as usual, sat on the first row of benches, a little to the left of Mr. D'Israeli, and so exceedingly anxious was the right honourable baronet to encourage the *débutant* to proceed, that he repeatedly turned round his head, and, looking the youthful orator in the face, cheered him in the most stentorian tones . . .

At one time, in consequence of the extraordinary interruptions he met with, Mr. D'Israeli intimated his willingness to resume his seat, if the House wished him to do so. He proceeded, however, for a short time longer, but was still assailed by groans and under-growls in all their varieties; the uproar, indeed, often became so great as completely to drown his voice . . .

The exhibition altogether was a most extraordinary one. Mr. D'Israeli's appearance and manner were very singular. His dress also was peculiar: it had much of a theatrical aspect. His black hair was long and flowing, and he had a most ample crop of it.

James Grant, *The British Senate in 1838* (London, 1838).

His Views on Marriage

May 22, 1833

15 By the bye, would you like Lady Z.......... for a sister-in-law, very clever, 25,000l., and domestic? As for 'love', all my friends who married for love and beauty either beat their wives or live apart from them. This is literally the case. I may commit many follies in life, but I never intend to marry for 'love', which I am sure is a guarantee of infelicity.

Lord Beaconsfield's Correspondence with His sister, 1832–1852, ed. Ralph Disraeli (John Murray, 1886).

Ben Marries

16   Sir Wyndham Lewis had a wife;
                But stupid-like, Sir Wyndham died,

And left her lonesome in the strife
Of this most miserable life,
So she became Ben's bride

Her weight I can't exactly gauge.
Nor can I tell her tale of years;
But she was over Dizzy's age
By fifteen summers, I'll engage,
Tho' such a tale appears!

For who could fancy Ben would choose
A woman much his senior
With whom to tie th' eternal noose?
But then you know 'tis like the Jews
To value golden ore!

And she possessed a mass of coin
That made her younger by a score:
And all but rendered her divine!
The daughter of old Pluto's line,
The God whom most adore! . . .

'Ha! Ha!' said Dizzy—'I want power!
What gives it? what but yellow coin?
Good! I may clasp it any hour
For that dear widow has a dower,
And she is wholly mine.'

James George Ashworth, *Imperial Ben, A Jew d'esprit*
(Remington & Co., 1879).

Sybil, or the Two Nations

17 The situation of the rural town of Marney* was one of the
most delightful easily to be imagined. In a spreading dale,
contiguous to the margins of a clear and lively stream, surrounded by meadows and gardens, and backed by lofty hills
undulating and richly wooded, the traveller on the opposite
heights of the dale would often stop to admire the merry
prospect, that recalled to him the traditional epithet of his
country.

Beautiful illusion! For behind that laughing landscape

* An imaginary town, though Disraeli's description was based on personal
observation. in the north and Government blue books. His picture is not exaggerated.

penury and disease fed upon the vitals of a miserable population . . . Marney mainly consisted of a variety of narrow and
crowded lanes formed by cottages built of rubble, or unhewn
stones without cement, and from age, or badness of the
material, looking as if they could scarcely hold together. The
gaping chinks admitted every blast; the leaning chimneys had
lost half their original height; the rotten rafters were evidently
misplaced; while in many instances the thatch, yawning in
some parts to admit the wind and wet, and in all utterly unfit
for its original purpose of giving protection from the weather,
looked more like the top of a dunghill than a cottage. Before
the doors of these dwellings, and often surrounding them, ran
open drains full of animal and vegetable refuse, decomposing
into disease, or sometimes in their imperfect course filling foul
pits or spreading into stagnant pools, while a concentrated
solution of every species of dissolving filth was allowed to soak
through and thoroughly impregnate the walls and ground
adjoining.

These wretched tenements seldom consisted of more than
two rooms, in one of which the whole family, however numerous, were obliged to sleep, without distinction of age, or sex, or
suffering. With the water streaming down the walls, the light
distinguished through the roof, with no hearth even in winter,
the virtuous mother in the sacred pangs of childbirth gives
forth another victim to our thoughtless civilisation;
surrounded by three generations whose inevitable presence is
more painful than her sufferings in that hour of travail; while
the father of her coming child, in another corner of the sordid
chamber, lies stricken by that typhus which his contaminating
dwelling has breathed into his veins, and for whose next prey is
perhaps destined his new-born child. These swarming walls
had neither windows nor doors sufficient to keep out the
weather, or admit the sun or supply the means of ventilation;
the humid and putrid roof of thatch exhaling malaria like all
other decaying vegetable matter. The dwelling rooms were
neither boarded nor paved; and whether it were that some
were situate in low and damp places, occasionally flooded by
the river, and usually much below the level of the road; or that
the springs, as was often the case, would burst through the
mud floor; the ground was at no time better than so much
clay, while sometimes you might see little channels cut from
the centre under the doorways to carry off the water, the door

itself removed from its hinges: a resting place for infancy in its deluged home. These hovels were in many instances not provided with the commonest conveniences of the rudest police; contiguous to every door might be observed the dungheap on which every kind of filth was accumulated, for the purpose of being disposed of for manure, so that, when the poor man opened his narrow habitation in the hope of refreshing it with the breeze of summer, he was met with a mixture of gases from reeking dunghills.

This town of Marney was a metropolis of agricultural labour, for the proprietors of the neighbourhood having for the last half-century acted on the system of destroying the cottages on their estates, in order to become exempted from the maintenance of the population, the expelled people had flocked to Marney, where, during the war, a manufactory had afforded them some relief, though its wheels had long ceased to disturb the waters of the Mar.

Deprived of this resource, they had again gradually spread themselves over that land which had as it were rejected them; and obtained from its churlish breast a niggardly subsistence. Their re-entrance into the surrounding parishes was viewed with great suspicion; their renewed settlement opposed by every ingenious contrivance; those who availed themselves of their labour were careful that they should not become dwellers on the soil; and though, from the excessive competition, there were few districts in the kingdom where the rate of wages was more depressed, those who were fortunate enough to obtain the scant remuneration, had, in addition to their toil, to endure each morn and even a weary journey before they could reach the scene of their labour, or return to the squalid hovel which profaned the name of home.

*   *   *

'There is so much to lament in the world in which we live,' said the younger of the strangers, 'that I can spare no pang for the past' . . .

'It is a community of purpose that constitutes society,' continued the younger stranger, 'without that men may be drawn into contiguity, but they still continue virtually isolated.'

'And is that their condition in cities?'

'It is their condition everywhere; but in cities that condition is aggravated . . . In great cities men are brought together by the desire of gain. They are not in a state of co-operation, but of isolation, as to making of fortunes; and for all the rest they are careless of neighbours. Christianity teaches us to love our neighbour as ourself; modern society acknowledges no neighbour.'

'Well, we live in strange times,' said Egremont, struck by the observation of his companion . . .

'When the infant begins to walk, it also thinks that it lives in strange times,' said his companion.

'Your inference?' asked Egremont.

'That society, still in its infancy, is beginning to feel its way.'

'This is a new reign,' said Egremont, 'perhaps it is a new era.'

'I think so,' said the younger stranger.

'I hope so,' said the older one.

'Well, society may be in its infancy,' said Egremont slightly smiling; 'but, say what you like, our Queen reigns over the greatest nation that ever existed.'

'Which nation?' asked the younger stranger, 'for she reigns over two.'

The stranger paused; Egrement was silent, but looked inquiringly.

'Yes,' resumed the younger stranger after a moment's interval. 'Two nations; between whom there is no intercourse and no sympathy; who are as ignorant of each other's habits, thoughts and feelings, as if they were dwellers in different zones, or inhabitants of different planets; who are formed by a different breeding, are fed by different food, are ordered by different manners, and are not governed by the same laws.'

'You speak of—' said Egremont, hesitatingly.

'THE RICH AND THE POOR.'

Benjamin Disraeli, *Sybil, or the Two Nations* (London, 1845).

Disraeli attacks Peel

18 *May 21, 1846*

Last week the debate in the House of Commons came to a close at last, wound up by a speech of Disraeli's, very clever, in which he hacked and mangled Peel with the most unsparing severity, and positively tortured his victim.* It was a miserable and degrading spectacle. The whole mass of the Protectionists cheered him with vociferous delight, making the

* See pp. 20–1.

roof ring again, and when Peel spoke, they screamed and hooted at him in the most brutal manner. When he vindicated himself, and talked of honour and conscience, they assailed him with shouts of derision and gestures of contempt . . . They hunt him like a fox, and they are eager to run him down and kill him in the open, and they are full of exultation at thinking they have nearly accomplished this object.

Charles Greville, *The Greville Memoirs* (Longmans, Green, 1885).

In Office

19 *February 21, 1852*
Went to Disraeli's after breakfast, and found him in a state of delight at the idea of coming into office. He said he 'felt just like a young girl going to her first ball,' constantly repeating, 'Now we have got a *status*'. With all his apparent apathy when attacked in the House of Commons, he is always, when out of it, in the highest state of elation or lowest depth of despair, according to the fortune of the day.

Lord Malmesbury, *Memoirs of an Ex-Minister* (Longmans, Green, 1884).*

Attacked in Quarterly Review

20 To crush the Whigs by combining with the Radicals was the first and last maxim of Mr. Disraeli's Parliamentary tactics. He had never led the Conservatives to victory as Sir Robert Peel had led them to victory. He had never procured the triumphant assertion of any Conservative principle, or shielded from imminent ruin any ancient institution. But he had been a successful leader to this extent, that he had made any Government, while he was in opposition, next to an impossibility. His tactics were so various, so flexible, so shameless—the net by which his combinations were gathered in was so wide—he had so admirable a knack of enticing into the same lobby a happy family of proud old Tories and foaming Radicals, martial squires jealous for their country's honour, and manufacturers who had written it off their books as an unmarketable commodity—that so long as his party backed

* Earl of Malmesbury, (1807–1899), who was Foreign Secretary at the same time as Disraeli was Chancellor of the Exchequer in Lord Derby's government in 1852.

him, no Government was strong enough to hold out against his attacks. They might succeed in repelling this sally or that; but sooner or later their watchful and untiring enemy, perfectly reckless from what quarter or in what uniform he assaulted, was sure to find out the weak point at which the fortress could be scaled . . .

They were never reduced, as under the Fabian guidance of Sir Robert Peel, to look for their sole hope of office in the slowly swelling aggregate of votes, that indicated year by year the gradual growth of the Conservative reaction. Their new chief kept up their spirit by a less scrupulous and more venturesome game . . . For their hopes of success they only waited upon that Providence that maketh Radicals to rebel . . . The Conservatives could not blind themselves to the fact that their leaders held office not because Conservatism was preferred by the House of Commons, but because the Radicals wished to punish the Whigs for not being Radical enough.

'The Budget and the Reform Bill', *The Quarterly Review,* April, 1860.*

Disraeli to the Rescue

21 Let the Conservative party never forget the hopeless Slough of Despond in which they were wallowing when kind fortune sent them Mr. DISRAELI for a leader . . . They had grown weary of a chief** who was too liberal for their contracted views of national policy, and avenged themselves upon him by an act of renunciation which left them without leaders, and apparently at the mercy of their opponents. They were irretrievably committed to a cause the very worst and most unpopular to which a party ever sacrificed its honours and its prospects . . .

Gradually, almost imperceptibly, Mr DISRAELI has weaned his party from their most flagrant errors . . . He has taught them a lesson which they have been slow indeed to learn . . . He has taught them to profess, at any rate, and probably to feel, a sympathy for the great body of their countrymen, and to recognise the necessity of looking to opinion for support. When he found the Tory party they were

* The article, published anonymously, was written by Lord Robert Cecil, later the Marquis of Salisbury, a Conservative Prime Minister.
** i.e. Sir Robert Peel.

armed in impenetrable prejudice; under him they have become no longer an impediment, but competitors with the Liberals in the career of progress.
The Times, June 6, 1860.

The Second Reform Bill

22 But, now, is this to be a long job, this considering the Lords' amendments? They are numerous, and some very important. But let us hope two nights will suffice. On Monday grouse-shooting will begin. If possible, we must finish on Friday night, so that the sportsmen may leave town on Saturday for the moors. Two nights then, we said, must settle this business. 'But it was settled in one.' Not long after midnight my Lords' amendments had been debated, the question thereon put, and the decision given. Such rapid work as this has scarcely ever been paralleled. This rapidity was mainly owing to the skill, and tact, and reticence of the leader of the House [Disraeli]. He opened the evening with a speech announcing the policy of the Government. His speech was short and compact, and after that he scarcely uttered a word during the whole night. He wanted rapidity of action, and not a war of words; and knowing well that talk is prolific of talk, that one speech often breeds a dozen, he sat and listened, and was silent. . . . Indeed, scarcely a man of the party spoke all the night . . . From the Treasury bench came no sound; and the Conservative phalanx, massed behind their leader, were silent, except that they now and then cheered and groaned . . . And this is how it happened that we did the work of two nights in one. It must be certainly placed to the credit of the Conservative leader. And here let us notice that it is not the first time that he has developed this remarkable talent for silence. It has been conspicuous ever since he took office, and most conspicuous whilst steering the Reform Bill through the House. . . .

It has been remarked that, whatever may have been done in the Cabinet, in the House, the leader appeared to consult none of his colleagues. We noticed in our last that Disraeli had secured a private room out of the precincts of the House, and it may be imagined that there councils of war assembled. We, however, doubt it. At all events, generally no one was present there with the Conservative chief but his private secretary, Mr. Corry, and Mr. Lambert, of the Poor Law

Board, who has had so much to do in framing the Bill. In short, Disraeli has steered this Bill through himself; alone he did it; and with what wonderful skill none but those who watched him from night to night can know . . . The man that conquered all these difficulties has no superior, and scarcely an equal, in Parliamentary history. In short, whatever we may think of him, he is a very clever fellow.

William White, *The Inner Life of the House of Commons* (T. Fisher Unwin, 1897).*

Purchase of Suez Canal Shares

23 The purchase, however, was a rather formidable job. Lord Derby, the Foreign Minister, did not like it; the Chancellor of the Exchequer, Sir Stafford Northcote, did not like it . . . Undoubtedly some very grave considerations had to be faced. I had heard that shortly, perhaps within a few hours, the Khedive's canal shares,** which amounted to nearly a half of them, would pass into French hands. Many politicians in this country had always disliked or mistrusted the Suez Canal scheme; one result of which was that the property was nearly all French. Very little of the Suez Canal stock was held out of France at that time . . . At that time about 86 per cent of the tonnage that passed through the canal was British. The British merchant, therefore, was paying the dividends, the French public was receiving them. The consequence of this was that the canal dues were kept very high . . .

I asked Lord Derby to consider what the chances of ever getting the canal dues lowered would be if the whole of the property, and not half of it, passed into the hands of the French . . . Then arose another question. What authority or what means had the Government for buying shares in a commercial company? Parliament was not sitting, and even if it was and the House of Commons were asked for this £4,000,000, 'the gaff would be blown,' to use Lord Derby's own phrase. (Laughter) The French would immediately be on the *qui vive* . . .

The money question was of instant importance, but that was

---

* William White, (1807–1882), principal door-keeper at the House of Commons: like many such officials his judgements were often sounder than those of some of his more distinguished masters.

** The Khedive of Egypt, who was on the verge of bankruptcy, had 44 per cent of the shares in the Suez Canal Company.

virtually settled when Lord Rowton* was sent by Mr. Disraeli to Baron Rothschild; although at first the Baron must have been rather staggered at being asked to supply four millions in a very few days without any security. (Laughter). But the money was furnished, though not all at once. I believe it was paid in instalments. The whole business occupied no more than eight or ten days. Not a whisper got out, nobody heard a word of what was going on, and there came a Friday when the air of England was filled with thrown-up hats. (Cheers) All England acclaimed the great achievement which would redound for ever to the honour of Mr. Disraeli.

Mr. Greenwood's Speech in Honouring Frederick Greenwood, being speeches delivered in praise of him at a dinner held on April 8, 1905 (Privately Printed, 1905).**

The Queen 'in ecstasies'

24 *November 25, 1875*—To Lady Bradford
After a fortnight of the most unceasing labor and anxiety, I (for between ourselves, and ourselves only, I may be egotistical in this matter)—I have purchased for England, the Khedive of Egypt's interest in the Suez Canal.

We have had all the gamblers, capitalists, financiers of the world, organised and platooned in bands of plunderers, arrayed against us, and secret emissaries in every corner, and have baffled them all, and have never been suspected.

The day before yesterday, Lesseps, whose Company has the remaining shares, backed by the French Government, whose agent he was, made a great offer. Had it succeeded, the whole of the Suez Canal would have belonged to France, and they might have shut it up!

We have given the Khedive 4 millions sterling for his interest, and run the chance of Parliament supporting us. We could not call them together for the matter, for that would have blown everything to the skies, or to Hades.

The Faery*** is in ecstasies about 'this great and important event'.

* Disraeli's private secretary.
** Frederick Greenwood, (1830–1909), editor of the *Pall Mall Gazette*, who suggested the purchase of the Suez Canal shares to Disraeli, though his claims to have been the first to do so has sometimes been disputed.
*** Disraeli's private nick-name for Queen Victoria—from Spenser's *Faery Queen*.

The Letters of Disraeli to Lady Bradford and Lady Chesterfield, ed. The Marquis of Zetland (Ernest Benn, 1929).*

Empress of India

Extracts from the Queen's Journal

25 WINDSOR CASTLE, *26th February, 1876.*—A very fine morning . . . After luncheon saw Mr. Disraeli, who talked of the Titles Bill** causing trouble and annoyance, he could not tell why. I spoke of the feeling about the Colonies and gave him full power to add anything to the title. He thought a plan of his to give to two of my sons the titles of Duke of Canada and Duke of Australia might be a good way of solving the difficulty, and I saw no objection to it if he found it would be of use. . . .

WINDSOR CASTLE, *17th March, 1876.*—Heard on getting up, that the second reading of the Titles Bill had been carried by 105!—an immense majority. It is to be hoped now no more stupid things will be said, and that the matter will be dropped . . . All sensible people know that this Bill will make *no* difference here, and that I am all for it, as it is so important for India. There is no feeling whatever in the country against it, but the Press took it up, having at first been all the other way.

WINDSOR CASTLE, *25th April, 1876.*—Saw Mr. Disraeli at one. He was much annoyed at what had occurred about the Titles Bill, which certainly seemed inexplicable. Speaking of the Proclamation, he explained that it had been most carefully considered, that the title was not to be used in writs and other legal matters in England, or in ordinary transactions, but would be for commissions in the Army, as officers served in India as well as in England, also in all foreign treaties and communications with foreign Sovereigns. In these cases I should have to sign 'Victoria R. & I.'

The Letters of Queen Victoria, Second Series, ed. George Earle Buckle (John Murray, 1926).

---

* A few months after his wife's death, Disraeli who always felt a very great need of female companionship, fell in love with the Countess of Bradford, who was then fifty-four. He wrote her and her sister, Countess of Chesterfield, many hundreds of letters.

** The Royal Titles Act which made the Queen Empress of India.

EMPRESS AND EARL;

OR, ONE GOOD TURN DESERVES ANOTHER.

Lord Beaconsfield. "THANKS, YOUR MAJESTY! I MIGHT HAVE HAD IT BEFORE! *NOW* I THINK I HAVE *EARNED* IT!"

'By Jingo'

26   We don't want to fight, but, by Jingo if we do,
       We've got the ships, we've got the men, we've got the
          money too.
       We've fought the Bear before,
       And while Britons shall be true
       The Russians shall not have Constantinople.
       Music Hall Song, composed by G. W. Hunt and sung by
       G. H. MacDermott, (1877).

'Peace with Honour'

27 As soon as the packet which was bringing back the two
English plenipotentiaries touched the pier at Dover, the
Mayor and Corporation stepped on board to present the
Premier with a congratulatory address. The Premier in making
his acknowledgements, claimed to have brought back 'Peace
with Honour' . . . and demanded recognition for Lord
Salisbury's* share in this result as equal to his own.

   Other addresses of welcome and congratulation followed,
and Ministers proceeded by special train to London. The
Charing Cross Station had been decorated in their honour,
and was crowded with spectators who closely packed the tiers
of seats which had been erected. The arrival of the Ministers
was greeted with ringing cheers. They were received upon the
platform by the Lord Mayor and Sheriffs, in their robes of
office, and a distinguished company. Something of the air of a
triumph was given to their progress along the crowded way to
Downing Street.

   In response to the cheers of the throng Lord Beaconsfield
appeared at a window, and repeated the phrase which he had
used at Dover . . .

   On July 22nd, Lord Beaconsfield was invested with the
Order of the Garter. On Saturday the 27th the two Ministers
were entertained at a banquet given by a numerous body of
Conservative peers and members of the House of Commons.
The entertainment was held in the Duke of Wellington's
Riding School at Knightsbridge, as the only building in the
West End which could afford sufficient accommodation. Con-
spicuous among the mottoes with which the hall was decorated

   * The Foreign Secretary who played a major role in the negotiations of the Congress
of Berlin.

was 'Peace with Honour'. On August 3rd the Premier and Foreign Secretary were presented with the Freedom of the City of London at the Guildhall, and in the evening they were entertained by the Lord Mayor at a banquet at the Mansion House.

Geo. Carslake Thompson, *Public Opinion and Lord Beaconsfield, 1875–1880* (Macmillan, 1886).

Newspaper's praise

28 Today, at the close of a long and doubtful struggle, a still more extraordinary success crowns the career of the Prime Minister. He returns from discharging the office of chief Plenipotentiary of England in the most important and most critical negotiation of our time, and he has discharged it to the satisfaction of his own country and with the general applause of Europe. He has, at all events, averted a terrible war; he has, at the same time, maintained the dignity and the authority of his country; and he has in all probability established affairs in the East upon a basis on which a really stable edifice may be erected. Lord Beaconsfield will be welcomed in London today as the chief actor in one of the most honourable triumphs in the modern diplomacy of England.

The Times, July 16, 1878.

Acquisition of Cyprus

29 *Extracts from the Queen's Journal*
OSBORNE, *20th July, 1878.*—Went out to tea with Beatrice* and remained reading and writing till near 7, when I went in to see Lord Beaconsfield, who had just arrived. He looked well, was in excellent spirits and had a great deal to tell. The difficulties were very great at first. Bismarck, though very Prussian, was an extraordinary man, who talked very loosely and carelessly about everything, most original and peculiar; delighted at our taking Cyprus, as that was *taking something…* The Russians were very sore about Cyprus, at least all but Schouvaloff. At one moment, Lord Beaconsfield had to threaten to break up the Congress, and even let it be known his special train was ordered, thereby carrying the point which the Russians wanted to resist.

The Letters of Queen Victoria, Second Series, ed. George Earle Buckle (John Murray, 1926).

* Princess Beatrice, (1857–1944), the Queen's youngest daughter.

Occupation of Cyprus

30 Now you will at once see that it is very important that England should be able to protect the road to India. Your map will very likely have the British Possessions all over the world coloured *red*. Then you will see that, along that *road to India*, England has *four* small but important colonies. These are *Gibraltar*, at the *entrance* of the Mediterranean; *Malta*, in the *middle*; *Cyprus*, at the *east-end*; and *Aden*, at the entrance to the *Red Sea* . . .

The circumstances attending the acquisition of Cyprus were these: a war between Russia and Turkey had just concluded, in which Russia had been victorious, and had taken from Turkey considerable territory in Asia Minor.

Now there are various reasons why England would be very sorry to see Russia all-powerful in Asia Minor. So the English Government made an agreement with Turkey, by which Turkey gave up to England the Island of Cyprus; and England in return undertook to defend Turkey against Russia in Asia Minor. . . .

Cyprus. . . . was taken possession of on the 22nd July 1878, by *Sir Garnet Wolseley* as Lord High Commissioner.

Unfortunately the season proved a very unhealthy one; and as no sanitary precautions were taken, a troublesome fever broke out among the troops landed there. Opinion is still much divided as to the wisdom of its occupation; but there is little doubt that it will ultimately become an important British military station, such as Malta now is.

T. S. Taylor, *First Principles of Modern History, 1815–1879, from the English Point of View* (Relfe Brothers, London, n.d.).*

Victoria's Tribute

31 The coffin lies on its bier in an alcove leading out of the modest hall of Hughenden Manor. But of its material, one might almost say of its dimensions, nothing can be seen. It is literally one mass of floral beauty. Here are wreaths from every member of the Royal Family in England—bouquets of primroses sent by the Queen, with an inscription attached to them, say-

---

* T. S. Taylor, author of a number of schoolbooks on different topics between 1877 and 1892.

ing that they came from Osborne Hill,* and that they are of the sort which Lord Beaconsfield loved. Here are garlands of gardenias and camellias, of rose-buds and Lent lilies, of crocus, and hyacinth, and daffodil... As each visitor enters the drawing-room he is received by Lord Rowton, who utters, however, only a few words, and those with baited breath. Ambassadors, statesmen, diplomatists, cabinet ministers, past, present, and future; country gentlemen who years ago occupied a seat in the House of Commons, but who have since retired, and who probably have no intention of returning to parliamentary life; professional men—doctors, lawyers, and *littérateurs*—are all here together . . .

On the following Saturday, April 30th, the Queen, accompanied by Princess Beatrice, paid a visit to the tomb of the late Earl of Beaconsfield, and the vault, which was again reopened to receive the royal offerings of affectionate respect, was afterwards finally closed. The visit of Her Majesty was intended to be strictly private, and the secret was most faithfully kept by the few to whom it was confided. On Thursday Lord Rowton was summoned to Windsor, when the Queen intimated her desire to visit Hughenden churchyard and lay on the coffin of the deceased Earl another wreath. The Queen also wished to follow the exact route travelled by Lord Beaconsfield on his last return from Windsor to Hughenden, and to traverse the exact course of the bier on the day of the funeral from the Manor House to the tomb . . . Arrangements were made for securing the desired privacy without exciting public curiosity, which for several days past has been very sensitive in the district in consequence of the trench leading to the vault not having been completely filled in. Rumour accounted for the fact by asserting that an iron door to close the aperture was in course of construction, and when the masons were employed on Saturday to re-open the trench, it was generally believed that this was the case . . .

After ten minutes' stay within the church, the Royal visitors walked across the greensward to the inclined excavation leading to the opening to the vault. They were followed by the Queen's personal attendant, who carried a beautiful wreath and cross, formed of white camellias and other flowers, exquisitely worked in porcelain, brought in the Royal carriage

* In the grounds of Osborne House, Isle of Wight, one of the Queen's favourite residences, where she died in 1901.

from Windsor Castle. For a few seconds Her Majesty paused at the head of the incline and stood looking sorrowfully down the sloping path at the open vault. Then, followed by Princess Beatrice, Lord Rowton, the Lady in Waiting, and Lord Charles Fitzroy, Her Majesty walked into the tomb and placed the wreath and cross upon the heap of floral offerings, which completely obscured the lid of Lord Beaconsfield's coffin. . . .

When, at last, the sad visit was concluded the Queen and Princess Beatrice emerged slowly from the excavation, and, walking to their carriage, drove from the churchyard, some heavy drops of rain falling as the Royal party proceeded up the steep and winding roadway on the hillside to the small plateau on which the residence of the late Lord Beaconsfield is situated . . . Before their departure for London, Lord Rowton and Sir Philip Rose returned to the churchyard, and saw that the masonry work for finally closing the vault was far advanced, Her Majesty having expressed a desire that the vault should not again be opened.

Memorials of Lord Beaconsfield, Reprinted from the *Standard* (Macmillan & Co., 1881).

Gladstone's Public View

32 There were other great qualities, not intellectual . . . qualities immediately connected with conduct—with regard to which I should say, were I a younger man, I should like to stamp the recollection of them upon my mind, for my own future guidance, and with regard to which I will say, to those younger than myself, that I would strongly recommend them for notice and imitation. These characteristics were not only written in a marked manner on his career, but were possessed by him in a degree undoubtedly extraordinary. I speak, for example, of his strength of will, his long-sighted persistency of purpose, reaching from his first entrance on the avenue of life to its very close, his remarkable power of self-government, and last, not least, his great Parliamentary courage, which I, who have been associated in the course of my life with some scores of Ministers, have never seen surpassed.

Mr. Gladstone's speech on A Monument to the Earl of Beaconsfield, May 9, 1881, (Hansard, 1881).

Gladstone's Private View

33 Mr. G[ladstone].—He insisted that democracy had certainly not saved us from a distinct decline in the standard of public men. . . . Look at the whole conduct of opposition from '80 to '85—every principle was flung overboard, if they could manufacture a combination against the government. For all this deterioration one man and one man alone is responsible, Disraeli. He is the grand corrupter. He it was who sowed the seed.

J[ohn] M[orley]—Ought not Palmerston to bear some share in this? Mr. G.—No, no; Pam had many strong and liberal convictions . . . A curious irony, was it not, that it should have fallen to me to propose a motion for a memorial both to Pam. and Dizzy?

John Morley, *The Life of William Ewart Gladstone* (Macmillan & Co., 1906).*

LATER ASSESSMENTS

English by Adoption

34 In this high sense of the word, Lord Beaconsfield cannot be called great, either as a man of letters or as a statesman. *Vivian Grey*** is nothing but a loud demand on his contemporaries to recognise how clever a man has appeared among them. In every one of his writings there is the same defect, except in *Sybil* and in *Lothair* . . .***

Thus it was perhaps no public man in England ever rose so high and acquired power so great, so little of whose work has survived him. Not one of the great measures which he once insisted on did he carry or attempt to carry. The great industrial problems are still left to be solved by the workmen in their own unions. Ireland is still in the throes of disintegration. If the colonies have refused to be cast loose from us their continued allegiance is not due to any effort of his. From Berlin he brought back peace with honour, but if peace

* John Morley, (1838–1923), first Viscount, journalist, author, and statesman, a firm supporter of Gladstonian policies, who served as Irish Secretary under Gladstone in 1886 and from 1892 to 1895.

** Disraeli's first novel published anonymously in 1826, though it was soon well-known that he was the author.

*** *Sybil*, published 1845, and *Lothair*, published 1870—two of his best-known novels.

remains the honour was soon clouded. The concessions which he prided himself on having extorted are evaded or ignored, and the imperial spirit which he imagined that he had awakened sleeps in indifference . . . Of all those great achievements there remain only to the nation the Suez Canal shares and the possession of Cyprus, and to his Queen the gaudy title of Empress of India. What is there besides? Yet there is a relative greatness as well as an absolute greatness . . . Disraeli said of Peel that he was the greatest member of Parliament that there had ever been.* He was himself the *strongest* member of Parliament in his own day, and it was Parliament which took him as its foremost man and made him what he was. No one fought more stoutly when there was fighting to be done; no one knew better when to yield, or how to encourage his followers. He was a master of debate. He had perfect command of his temper, and while he ran an adversary through the body he charmed even his enemies by the skill with which he did it. . . . But he was English only by adoption, and he never completely identified himself with the country which he ruled. At heart he was a Hebrew to the end, and of all his triumphs perhaps the most satisfying was the sense that a member of that despised race had made himself the master of the fleets and armies of the proudest of Christian nations . . .

If he was ambitious his ambition was a noble one. It was for fame and not for fortune. To money he was always indifferent. He was even ostentatious in his neglect of his own interests. Though he left no debts behind him, in his life he was always embarrassed.

J. A. Froude, *The Earl of Beaconsfield*, new ed. J. M. Dent, 1905).**

A Thorough Oriental

35 No one who has lived much in the East can . . . fail to be struck with the fact that Disraeli was a thorough Oriental. The taste for tawdry finery, the habit of enveloping in mystery matters as to which there was nothing to conceal, the love of intrigue, the tenacity of purpose—though this is perhaps more a Jewish than an invariably Oriental characteristic—the luxuriance of

** James Anthony Froude, (1818–1894), a prolific historian more distinguished for his literary ability than his judgement.

the imaginative faculties, the strong addiction to plausible generalities set forth in florid language, the passionate outbursts of grief expressed at times in words so artificial as to leave a doubt in the Anglo-Saxon mind as to whether the sentiments can be genuine, the spasmodic eruption of real kindness of heart into a character steeped in cynicism, the excess of flattery accorded at one time to Peel for purely personal objects contrasted with the excess of vituperation poured forth on O'Connell for purposes of advertisement, and the total absence of any moral principle as a guide of life—all these features, in a character which is perhaps not quite so complex as is often supposed, hail from the East. What is not Eastern is his unconventionality, his undaunted moral courage, and his ready conception of novel political ideas—often specious ideas, resting on no very solid foundation, but always attractive, and always capable of being defended by glittering plausibilities. He was certainly a man of genius, and he used that genius to found a political school based on extreme self-seeking opportunism . . .

No tale of fiction is, indeed, more strange than that which tells how this nimble-witted alien adventurer, with his poetic temperament, his weird Eastern imagination and excessive Western cynicism, his elastic mind which he himself described as 'revolutionary', and his apparently wayward but in reality carefully regulated unconventionality, succeeded in spite of every initial disadvantage of race, birth, manners, and habits of thought, in dominating a proud aristocracy and using its members as so many pawns on the chess-board which he had arranged to suit his own purposes . . . Dealing with a class who honoured tradition, he startled the members of that class by shattering all the traditions which they had been taught to revere, and by endeavouring, with the help of specious arguments which many of them only half understood, to substitute others of an entirely novel character in their place . . .

The manner in which he proposed to reorganise our institutions was practically to render the middle classes politically powerless . . . He wished, above all things, to maintain the territorial magnates in the full possession of their properties. When he spoke of a 'union between the Conservative Party and the Radical masses' he meant a union between the 'patricians' and the working men . . .

The programme was foredoomed to failure, and the failure has been complete. Modern Conservatives can appeal to the middle classes, who . . . are their natural allies. They can also appeal to the working classes by educating them and by showing them that Socialism is diametrically contrary to their own interests. . . . They cannot advantageously masquerade in Radical clothes.

The Earl of Cromer, *Disraeli* (Macmillan, 1912).*

Loyal to the End

36 For the Conservative Party to fulfil its mission, it must retain the power of attracting into its ranks the young, able, and ambitious men of each succeeding generation, and of holding over the ministers of the day the constant possibility of a change. To do this they must be in a position not only to take office, but to keep it. And to place themselves in this position they must be ready to move with the times, and show themselves capable of satisfying the wants of the nation.

Lord Beaconsfield saw that this rule of action, so far from being a sacrifice of Conservative principles, was really the only way of giving effect to them. Changes which cannot be prevented may be rendered less destructive in Conservative hands than they would be in Radical hands; and Conservatives are acting just as honourable and dignified a part in adopting a policy of which they disapprove in the abstract, that they may render it less mischievous in the concrete, as they would be in resisting it altogether when their resistance is certain to be useless . . . With many Conservative Members of Parliament it is simply enough that they dislike a thing, that it seems to them intrinsically undesirable, to make them think it must be doggedly resisted without looking to the right or to the left. They do not consider that, in an age like the present, politics, from the Conservative point of view, are often but a choice of evils. They did not see this in times past, even if they see it now. But Lord Beaconsfield saw it, and proved his statesmanship by acting on it. . . .

Lord Beaconsfield has been called a 'political adventurer'. . . Surely a political adventurer, like a military adventurer, is one

* Evelyn Baring, first Earl of Cromer, (1841–1917), imperial administrator who as British Agent and Consul-General in Egypt virtually ruled that country between 1883 and 1907.

who makes his principles subservient to his interests, and transfers his allegiance from side to side as advantage or convenience dictates, indifferent to the cause which he is required to defend, and concerned only with the fulfilment of his duties and the receipt of his stipulated fee . . . Lord Beaconsfield never changed either his principles or his party. He was a Tory of the type which I have described, from the first address which he issued to the electors of High Wycombe to the last speech which he delivered in the House of Lords half a century afterwards. Insulted, distracted, and calumniated by the very men who should have been the first to welcome him, he never swerved for a moment in his attachment to the cause which he and they had at heart. He served the Tory party as no man except the younger Pitt had ever served it. He served it through poverty, adversity, and unpopularity, without ever losing heart or hope, or allowing his own private circumstances to affect his political conduct.

T. E. Kebbel, *Life of Lord Beaconsfield* (Cassell & Co. Ltd., 1888).

MODERN VIEWS

An English Patriot

37 It would not be true to think that he had no ideals at all and no objective other than climbing to the top of the greasy pole.

On the contrary, Disraeli was in a very real sense an English patriot, and a fervent believer in the greatness of his country; this fervour was all the stronger because he was himself something of an alien figure and, thanks to his origins and background, never quite belonged to the social and political world which he came to dominate. He equated England's greatness with the ascendancy of a particular class, the landed aristocracy which, though it also furnished its quota of Whig supporters, constituted the backbone of the Conservative Party throughout Disraeli's life . . .

What lasting effect, other than providing an eternal prototype of the romantic success story, did his career have on politics in his own day and thereafter? Perhaps the most important was the imprint which he left on his own party . . .

In the first place Disraeli decisively refuted the charge that the Conservatives were 'the stupid party'. Much could be said against him and his cabinet in 1874–80 but they could not be described as unintelligent. Nor could they be described as 'reactionary'. . .

Secondly, Disraeli made the Conservatives both the party of empire and the party of a strong, or as his enemies would have said, 'jingoistic' foreign policy. There was nothing inevitable about this development. In Palmerston's day those were the attributes of the Whig/Liberal Party rather than the Conservatives . . . From the early seventies onwards the Conservatives were identified with the cause of British nationalism, British ascendancy, and the pursuit of purely British interests without over-much consideration for those of other countries. For good or ill Disraeli, an alien outsider, had more responsibility for this than any other single individual.

Robert Blake, *Disraeli* (Oxford University Press, 1969).

A Timeless Quality

38 It is easy to underestimate Disraeli's innate conservatism . . . To think of him as a prisoner of the Tory party, a would-be Radical struggling to be free, is quite wrong . . .

After he became leader he had to make as many concessions and compromises and reversals as ever Peel had to make, but he was a more skilful politician than Peel. That is why he had a better Press from the politicians of both sides than from the administrators or the academic historians . . .

Where Disraeli excelled was in the art of presentation. He was an impresario and an actor manager. He was a superb parliamentarian, one of the half dozen greatest in our history . . .

. . . It is quite easy to imagine Disraeli living either today or in the era of Lord North. It is this timelessness that gives his best novels their lasting fascination, and makes his wit as good now as it was a hundred years ago. There is a champagne-like sparkle about him which has scarcely ever been equalled and never surpassed among statesmen.

Robert Blake, *Disraeli* (Eyre and Spottiswoode, 1966).

Consistent Opportunism

39 In 1865 he [Disraeli] was sixty-one, seven years younger than Derby. He had led the Conservative party in the House of Commons for nearly twenty years and had had remarkably

little success. He had led it as a party leader: he had led it with skill, with style and with self-control. He had kept it together in depression and expectation, but he had never had real power. Throughout the 'fifties and 'sixties, though it was often the largest single group in Parliament, Whig flexibility, Radical hostility to a wide range of Tory positions and Derby's reluctance at crucial moments had deprived it of the chance to govern. . . . His objective throughout these years was to create a credible government on a Tory base to replace the coalitions on Whig bases which had followed the fall of Peel. Though he cannot be said to have succeeded, he was attempting both to broaden and to deepen the Anglican and agrarian foundation onto which the party had forced itself in 1846.

The first thing to understand about Disraeli's policy between 1865 and 1867, therefore, is that its flexibility in relation to Catholic, Whig, Irish, Adullamite,* Liberal and Radical MPs was a continuation of one aspect of the policy he had adopted since he first had to combat the Russell/ Aberdeen/Palmerston coalitions in the 'fifties. The second thing to understand is that there is no reason to suppose that Disraeli knew in advance in 1865 which group he would be able most successfully to detach. . . .

Disraeli's was a policy of consistent opportunism—an attempt to be prepared for any chance that might arise to occupy as much of the central ground as he could, to hold out expectations to such Liberal or Irish groups as might be detached and to smooth down the rough edges of reactionary Toryism.

Maurice Cowling, *Disraeli, Gladstone and Revolution: The Passing of the Second Reform Bill* (Cambridge University Press, 1967).

Success overrated

40 As for the praise of conservatives in the twentieth century, there is a tendency, again, to interpret his success as a far more applicable conservatism than it really was. The truth is that Disraeli held the Conservative party together through a period of confusion in parliament. He enabled it to take office as a

---

* A name used in 1866 by John Bright to describe the Liberals led by E. Horsman and Robert Lowe, who opposed Liberal plans for parliamentary reform. The Cave of Adullam was where David gathered together all the discontented in his flight from Saul.

minority government three times in the fifties and the sixties, and in 1874 to form one of the first of the truly party ministries. But the making of the Conservative party, even the formation of the 1874 ministry, had to do with circumstances beyond Disraeli—with the death of Palmerston and the inevitable shift of his Conservative followers, with the disintegrating effect of Gladstone's leadership on the Liberals, with the dilemma of Liberalism in the twentieth century. Over these events Disraeli had little initiative or control.

Albert Tucker, 'Disraeli and the Natural Aristocracy', *The Canadian Journal of Economics and Political Science* (University of Toronto Press, February, 1962).

Retarded Development of Conservatism

41 There was no possibility of the party's going far along the 'Disraelian' road of popular appeal and social reform. Nor did Disraeli make very strenuous efforts to lead it in that direction. The popular Toryism of his youth had been in part a romantic extravaganza, in part a gesture against Peel, without much practical content, and after 1846 it was pushed into the background as he saw that the resumption of Peel's policy was the only viable course for his party. His coup of 1867 was not an attempt to re-establish the party's fortunes on the support of the masses, but a manoeuvre designed to break the Whig monopoly of the cause of constitutional progress, which the tactical situation forced him to carry further than he would have chosen . . .

Not until 1872 did he seriously attempt to make political capital out of support for the improvement of the social condition of the people. Then, indeed, he elevated social reform into one of the principal objects of his party. But he followed this with no concrete initiative or plan, and the imperialism which he proclaimed at the same time was in the end to be a more potent influence. . . . He did not found modern Conservatism; indeed, in destroying Peel, he had retarded its main line of development, the absorption of the bourgeoisie, by some twenty years. . . .

Modern Conservatism is essentially 'Peelite' in its structure and outlook, and it became so partly under Disraeli's auspices. But its striking electoral success since 1867 would have been impossible without its capacity to command a significant working-class vote, and here it owes something to Disraeli's sense of the necessity of accepting the enlargement of the political nation and making the social condition of the people one of the prime objects of the party's concern.

Paul Smith, *Disraelian Conservatism and Social Reform* (Routledge and Kegan Paul, 1967).

The Effects of the Berlin Treaty

42 The Berlin treaty was in one sense a turning point, for it left all the Balkan peoples, excepting the Albanians, with independent or autonomous states. On the other hand, an essential feature of the treaty was its disregard of ethnic and nationalist considerations. Disraeli from the beginning made it clear that he was interested in checking Russia, and not, as he put it, in creating 'an ideal existence for Turkish Xtians'. As a result, every one of the Balkan peoples was left thoroughly dissatisfied. The Bulgarians were embittered by the partition of their country, the Serbians by the administrative advance of Austria into Bosnia-Herzegovina, the Rumanians by the loss of southern Bessarabia, and the Greeks by their failure to obtain any territorial compensation . . . The direct and logical outcome of the Berlin settlement was the Serbian-Bulgarian War of 1885, the Bosnian crisis of 1908, the two Balkan Wars of 1912–1913, and the murder of Archduke Francis Ferdinand in 1914.

L. S. Stavrianos, *The Balkans, 1815–1914* (Holt, Rinehart and Winston, 1963).

As a Writer

43 How does one sum him up as a writer. Saintsbury,* who admired his novels, said nobody had ever quite known how to classify them; indeed, according to Lord David Cecil, 'for all their brilliance, they are not strictly speaking novels', and according to Leslie Stephen, 'he was not exactly a humourist, but something for which the rough nomenclature of critics has not yet provided a distinctive name'. Trollope** detested the

* George Saintsbury, (1845–1933), prominent critic and literary historian, who was professor of Rhetoric and English Literature at Edinburgh University from 1895 to 1915.

** Anthony Trollope, (1815–1882), Victorian novelist, who wrote a number of political novels, and a book on Palmerston.

whole body of his work . . . Of his prose fiction one can pronounce, uncontroversially, that, like his career, it is unique.

Paul Bloomfield, 'Disraeli', *Writers and their Work*, No. 138, (Longmans, Green & Co., 1961).

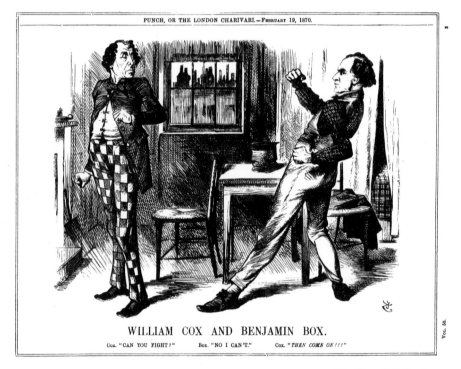

4. William Ewart Gladstone, 1809-1898

Gladstone was one of the major figures in nineteenth-century politics, but was he just an inconsistent humbug or a far-sighted statesman? Of all the British statesmen in the nineteenth century, he had the most complex character. He was self-opinionated, chopped down trees for exercise, and was so righteously absorbed in his work of rescuing prostitutes that he failed to realise that others might misunderstand the nature of his charitable work. It is possible that Queen Victoria's intense dislike of him in later years may have been caused partly by the rumours she heard about his nightly exercises (1-10).

Gladstone, the son of a Liverpool merchant, entered Parliament as a Tory M.P. in 1832. Although some of the 'stern and unbending Tories' had high hopes of him, he remained individualistic in his views all his life (11-13). In 1850 he strongly attacked Palmerston over the Don Pacifico affair (14). Two years later, he refused to serve under Derby in a Conservative government, and in the same year agreed to join Lord Aberdeen's coalition ministry of Whigs and Peelites—as Chancellor of the Exchequer. In 1853 he introduced the first of his famous series of Budgets which cut tariffs and reduced government expenditure (15-16). During the 1850s he made his final break with the Conservatives, refusing to serve under Derby again in 1858, and in the following year, agreeing to serve under Palmerston as Chancellor of the Exchequer. He remained in that post until 1865, though his relations with Palmerston were never very cordial (17).

On Palmerston's death in 1865 he became Liberal leader in the House of Commons and three years later prime minister for the first time. His first ministry (1868-1874) was distinguished for a number of important overdue reforms which had been blocked by Palmerston. Among them were reforms in Ireland, the country whose problems were to play such a large part in his latter life (18). The reforms created new sources of opposition to his government, which Disraeli exploited (19). In 1874, Disraeli came back into power and in the following year Gladstone resigned his leadership of the Liberal party (20).

But Gladstone could not keep out of the public eye for long. In 1876 he was back in public prominence with his attack on Turkish misrule in his pamphlet, *The Bulgarian Horrors and the Question of the East,* (21–23). In the 1880 election the Liberals came back into power, and Gladstone achieved a great personal victory with the first of his campaigns in his new constituency of Midlothian (24). Lord Granville and Lord Hartington gave up their leadership of the Liberal party and Gladstone became prime minister for the second time. Out of office, he was fond of making sweeping condemnations of foreign powers, and one of his first actions as prime minister was to apologise to Austria for some remarks he had made (25). During his second ministry, the Third Reform Bill was passed, but his government became discredited through defeats in the first Boer War and the death of Gordon at Khartoum (26–27). Gladstone undertook a second Midlothian campaign, but it was less successful than his first (28–29).

After a brief spell of Conservative rule under Lord Salisbury, Gladstone came back into power for the third time in February, 1886. By this time, he had become a convert to Home Rule for Ireland. His first Home Rule Bill was widely criticised and split the Liberal party (30–33). Gladstone decided to appeal to the country, but the Liberals were defeated in the election of July, 1886, and Gladstone resigned. But for many of the working and lower-middle classes in the country the Grand Old man could do no wrong and they still gave him their support (34).

From 1892 to 1894, Gladstone was in power again. His second Home Rule Bill passed the Commons but was defeated in the Lords and shortly afterwards, Gladstone resigned (42). He died in 1898 and was buried in Westminster Abbey on May 28.

In his own lifetime many people thought of him as an extremist; Queen Victoria described him once as a '*half-mad fire-brand*'. But those who knew him well understood that he was anything but a radical (35–38). Modern historians are even more conscious of his essential conservatism—and of the extremely important part that religion played in his life (39–42).

Further Reading

E. G. Collieu, *Gladstone* (Oxford University Press, 1968).
J. L. Hammond and M. R. D. Foot, *Gladstone and Liberalism* (English Universities Press, 1952).
Philip Magnus, *Gladstone*, A Biography (John Murray, 1954).

CHARACTER AND APPEARANCE

Careworn Expression

1 My recollections of him go back to the earlier sixties, when he was Chancellor of the Exchequer in Lord Palmerston's Government, and they become vivid at the point of time when he became Prime Minister—December, 1868.

In old age his appearance was impressive, through the combination of physical wear-and-tear with the unconquerable vitality of spirit which dwelt within. The pictures of him as a young man represent him as distinctly handsome, with masses of dark hair thrown back from a truly noble forehead, and eyes of singular expressiveness. But in middle life— and in his case middle life was continued till he was sixty—he was neither as good-looking as he once had been, nor as grand-looking as he eventually became. He looked much older than his age . . . His life had been, as he was fond of saying, a life of contention; and the contention had left its mark on his face, with its deep furrows and careworn expression . . .

In Gladstone's face, as I used to see it in those days, there was no look of gladness or victory. He had, indeed, won a signal triumph at the General Election of 1868, and had attained the supreme object of a politician's ambition. But he did not look the least as if he enjoyed his honours, but rather as if he felt an insupportable burden of responsibility. He knew that he had an immense amount to do in carrying the reforms which Palmerston had burked . . .

George W. E. Russell, *Prime Minister and Some Others* (T. Fisher Unwin, 1918).

Shooting Accident

2 Mr. Gladstone, as is well-known, early in life, lost a finger from the effects of an accident when out shooting. He always wore across the stump of the finger a black silk band, and at least on one occasion, when this evidence of the loss of his finger did not appear in a portrait, insisted on its insertion in the picture.

 J. G. Swift MacNeill, *W. E. Gladstone* (Swan Sonnenschein & Co, 1898).*

In the House of Commons

3 As usual when contemplating making a great speech, he had a flower in his buttonhole, and was dressed with unusual care. Striding swiftly past his colleagues on the Treasury Bench, he dropped into the seat kept vacant for him, and hastily taking up a copy of the Orders, ascertained what particular question in the long list had been reached. Then turning with a sudden bound of his whole body to the right, he entered into animated conversation with a colleague, his pale face working with excitement, his eyes glistening, and his right hand vehemently beating the open palm of his left as if he were literally pulverising an adversary. Tossing himself back with equally rapid gesture, he lay passive for the space of eighty seconds. Then, with another swift movement of the body, he turned to the colleague on the left, dashed his hand into his side pocket as if he had suddenly become conscious of a live coal secreted there, pulled out a letter, opened it with violent flick of extended forefingers, and earnestly discoursed thereon. . . .

 Often in angry debates one has seen him bounding about on the Front Bench apparently in uncontrollable rage, loudly ejaculating contradiction, violently shaking his head, and tendering other evidence of lost temper, hailed with hilarious laughter and cheers from gentlemen opposite. Finally springing to his feet with a fierce bound, he has stood at the table motionless and rigid, whilst the House rang with the tumult of cheers and the bray of hostile clamour. When the Speaker authorised his interruption it seemed as if the devil of unrest were thereby literally cast out. He suddenly became

* John Gordon Swift MacNeill, (1849–1926) professor of constitutional law, and Irish M.P. who supported Home Rule.

himself again, and in quiet voice set forth in admirably chosen language a weighty objection.
Henry W. Lucy, *The Right Honourable W. E. Gladstone* (W. H. Allen & Co., London, 1895).*

Lancashire Accent

4 Gladstone has a strong Lancashire accent; calls 'prefer' 'prefurr'; 'conform' almost becomes 'confurrm', but not, you understand, the Scottish 'r'. Occasionally, as old people will, he elides an h; 'erb, 'armony came as a surprise tonight.
C. R. L. F[letcher], *Mr. Gladstone at Oxford 1890* (Smith, Elder & Co., London, 1908).

A Poor Conversationalist

5 An absurd story has long been current among credulous people with rampant prejudices that Mr. Gladstone was habitally uncivil to the Queen. Now, it happens that Mr. Gladstone is the most courteous of mankind . . . It would therefore have been to the last degree improbable that he should make a departure from his usual habits in the case of a lady who was also his sovereign . . . He is so consumed by zeal for great subjects that he leaves out of account the possibility that they may not interest other people. He pays to every one, and not least to ladies, the compliment of assuming that they are on his own intellectual level, engrossed in the subjects which engross him, and furnished with at least as much information as will enable them to follow and to understand him. Hence the genesis of that absurd story about his demeanour to the Queen.

'He speaks to me as if I was a public meeting,' is a complaint which is said to have proceeded from illustrious lips. That most successful of all courtiers, the astute Lord Beaconsfield, used to engage her Majesty in conversation about water-colour drawing and the third-cousinships of German princes. Mr. Gladstone harangues her about the polity of the Hittites, or the harmony between the Athanasian Creed and Homer. The Queen, perplexed and uncomfortable, tries to make a digression—addresses a remark to a daughter or proffers

* Sir Henry William Lucy, (1845–1924), parliamentary writer and later editor of the Liberal paper, the *Daily News*, which ceased separate publication in 1930.

biscuit to a begging terrier. Mr. Gladstone restrains himself with an effort till the Princess has answered or the dog has sat down, and then promptly resumes: 'I was about to say—'. . .

For conversation, strictly so called, he has no turn. He asks questions when he wants information, and answers them copiously when asked by others. But of give-and-take, of meeting you half-way, of paying you back in your own conversational coin, he has little notion. He discourses, he lectures, he harangues. But if a subject is started which does not interest him it falls flat.

George W. E. Russell, *Collections and Recollections* (Thomas Nelson & Sons, n.d.).

Schoolmaster Manner

6 As he grew older, Gladstone became more intolerant of contradiction. One day when staying at Windsor Castle, he was being shown the Queen's China; taking up a plate which he believed to be Sèvres, he began a history of the manufactory there. A lady attached to the Court, a good judge of such things and who knew every piece in the Royal China Closet, ventured to point out that the plate was not made at Sèvres but at Dresden. Mr. Gladstone, angry at the interruption, turned to those present, and with the remark, 'as I was saying' gave them the whole story over again with manner and tone of a stern schoolmaster addressing unruly schoolboys.

Charles George Barrington, 'Political Recollections', *History Today* (August, 1961).

Rescue of Prostitutes

7 For more than forty years Gladstone devoted a great deal of his free time to the rescue of prostitutes. This work of mercy he shared with his wife, and it was the chief social and charitable enterprise in which he was engaged, becoming something more than mere welfare work, but almost a relaxation, or a way of life. It was not, however, the mission itself which was a source of gossip and innuendo, but the ways in which he set about it . . .

Many were the scurrilous broadsheets and smutty limericks written on this theme. Even during the 'Jack the Ripper' murders of the 'eighties* Gladstone's name was bandied in obscene verse. One such was:

Eight little whores, with no hope of heaven,
Gladstone may save one, then there'll be seven.
Seven little whores begging for a shilling,
One stays in Henage Court, then there's a killing. . . .

Gladstone himself was a great walker and he combined his daily—or more accurately nightly—exercise by making a habit of wandering alone in those districts where prostitution and street walkers flourished.

Policemen on the beat knew what he was doing, and it is perhaps not surprising that some of them cynically doubted whether his intentions were entirely charitable. Politicians, according to their party, regarded this work either with dismay or malicious delight . . .

Yet miraculously he survived and nobody in his lifetime dared openly to impugn his motives, or to make a public issue of his eccentricities.

Richard Deacon, *The Private Life of Mr. Gladstone* (Frederick Muller, 1965).

His Sense of Humour

8 Gladstone's tolerance of drunkenness was remarkable in one so austere. Hating a teetotal dinner, but having no temptation to drink hard, during his later years he appeared greatly to relish stories which hinged upon drunkenness. On the other hand, his repressions made any stories which hinged even remotely upon sex, virtually incomprehensible to him. Intimate friends occasionally tried to explain such stories to him in vain. Cynicism and irony invariably disgusted Gladstone, and his sense of humour was notoriously capricious. There were, however, two rather surprising stories which Gladstone could sometimes be persuaded to tell when he was in the right company, and in the right mood.

One concerned an Englishwoman in the Scottish Highlands who expressed regret when a local chieftain arrived at a party in Lowland dress, with trousers.

'Na, na, Lady! I never put on a kilt nowadays—except when I have taken physic.'

Sir Philip Magnus, *Gladstone* (John Murray, 1954).

* A series of murders of prostitutes in London by 'Jack the Ripper' whose identity has never been discovered.

His Amusements

9 In addressing a Meeting at Harrogate some years ago, Mr. A. Illingworth told the following story, 'A Government official having to wait on Mr. Gladstone expressed his sympathy with the Premier in having to sit out so may dreary hours' debate in the House of Commons, and inquired how he contrived to pass his time. Mr. Gladstone replied, "... I will show you what I do." Putting his hand into his pocket, he withdrew some papers, and added, "Last night we had a long debate, and I occupied the time in translating into Latin, as you see, the hymn, Rock of Ages".'
Rev. J. Brown, *Rock of Ages* (London, 1898).

Timber-Felling

10 *To the Right Hon. W. E. Gladstone, Esq., M.P., Hawarden Castle, Flintshire.*
Right Hon. Sir, A timber-feller who claims some celebrity in that line of business in Clay Cross, who is 54 years of age, is really, according to his age, considered one of the best timber-fellers in Derbyshire. His name is Hopkinson and he is particularly anxious to measure himself with Mr. Gladstone in that line, either in Hardwick Park, Chatsworth Park, or anywhere else as Mr. Gladstone thinks proper. He also desired me to say that he would stake a sovereign that his (Hopkinson's) tree would be down before Mr. Gladstone's tree, take them equal in circumference ... —Henry Clayton, Clay Cross.
Sir, I regard the challenge you have transmitted to me as a great compliment, but I at once give in. I never had pretensions to excellence, and if I had them by this time, from age and other causes, they would have been lost. I wish your friend may long enjoy his laurels.—W. E. Gladstone.
The Sheffield Telegraph, 1877, quoted in MacNeill, *op. cit.*

CONTEMPORARY VIEWS

Predictions of Trouble

11 The character of Gladstone, his extraordinary interest in theology, and his possible political future, were themes on which Dean Ramsay delighted to dilate. Although he had a sincere admiration for his friend, he said that he detected in

him a vein of vanity, and on one occasion I heard him utter a remarkable prophecy—it was when Mr. Gladstone quitted Sir Robert Peel's government on the question of Maynooth*— that William Gladstone would cause a good deal of trouble to a good many people before his career was over. Sir John Gladstone made a remark of a similar kind to my father . . . 'I am afraid my son's mind is such, my lord, that he will give a great many people the same trouble he has given Sir Robert.'
The Recollections of the Very Rev. G. D. Boyle, Dean of Salisbury (Edward Arnold, 1895).**

12 Sir,—Mr. Gladstone has recently been giving us lectures on conscience and conscientiousness; and this seems to me a fitting occasion to relate an incident which occurred in my own presence some years ago. I was dining at the table of a late Lord Chancellor . . . The Bishop*** was one of the party; and after dinner the conversation turned on Mr. Disraeli and Mr. Gladstone. Says the Lord Chancellor, 'Which of these two men do you think the most likely to be a cause of danger to England and its Constitution in the future?' The Bishop disposed of Mr. Disraeli with some sarcastic remarks to the effect that he did not apprehend much danger to England and its Constitution in the future from that gentleman's influence; 'but' he added slowly, 'Mr. Gladstone is another thing. You see he is a man who is believed by the mass of his countrymen to be a man of high principle who always acts and speaks strictly according to his conscience and in the manner he believes to be right at the time. Now,' he said 'such a man is, and must be, a great power for good or evil among that large class of our countrymen—honest, upright men—who do not think for themselves and who do not understand politics, but who put their confidence in some man whom they believe they can trust for principles and conscience.'

'But,' he concluded, 'those who know William Gladstone best know that he possesses a fatal facility of persuading himself that what is black today is white tomorrow; and a man

* Peel's Bill of 1845 to increase the grant to the Roman Catholic College at Maynooth in an attempt to conciliate the Catholic hierarchy in Ireland.
** George David Boyle, (1828–1901), son of a Scottish judge, Lord Boyle, and Dean of Salisbury from 1880 to his death.
*** Samuel Wilberforce, (1805–1873), at that time Bishop of Oxford, and later Bishop of Winchester, son of William Wilberforce, the reformer. A High Church Anglican, he was a personal friend of Gladstone.

with such an influence as he will command, and with such powers of self-persuasion, may come to be a serious danger to his country.'—One who Heard these remarks Made.
    'Letter in the St. James's Gazette', quoted in *Our Premier* (London, 1886).

'Stern, unbending Tory'

13 The author of this volume* is a young man of unblemished character, and of distinguished parliamentary talents, the rising hope of those stern and unbending Tories, who follow, reluctantly and mutinously, a leader,** whose experience and eloquence are indispensable to them, but whose cautious temper and moderate opinions they abhor. . . . We are much pleased . . . to see a grave and elaborate treatise on an important part of the Philosophy of Government proceed from the pen of a young man who is rising to eminence in the House of Commons. . . .
    Mr. Gladstone seems to us to be, in many respects, exceedingly well qualified for philosophical investigation [but] he has one gift most dangerous to a speculator,—a vast command of a kind of language, grave and majestic, but of vague and uncertain import . . . Mr. Gladstone's whole theory rests on this great fundamental proposition—that the Propagation of Religious Truth is one of the Principal Ends of Government, as government. This doctrine . . . is, that every association of human beings which exercises any power whatever—that is to say, every association of human beings—is bound, as such association, to profess a religion.
    It is perfectly true, that it would be a very good thing if all the members of all the associations in the world were men of sound religious views. . . . But it does not follow that every association of men must therefore, as such association, profess a religion. It is evident that many great and useful objects can be attained in this world only by co-operation. . . . Nothing seems to us more beautiful or more admirable in our social system, than the facility with which thousands of people, who perhaps agree only a single point, combine their energies for the purpose of carrying that single point. We see daily instances of this. Two men, one of them obstinately prejudiced

* *The Church and its Relations with the State*, by W. E. Gladstone, 1838.
** i.e. Sir Robert Peel.

against missions, the other president of a missionary society, sit together at the board of an hospital, and heartily concur in measures for the health and comfort of the patients. . . .
Lord Macaulay, *The Edinburgh Review*, April, 1839.*

Don Pacifico

14 Sir, great as is the influence and power of Britain, she cannot afford to follow, for any length of time, a self-isolating policy. It would be a contravention of the law of nature and of God, if it were possible for any single nation of Christendom to emancipate itself from the obligations which bind all other nations, and to arrogate, in the face of mankind, a position of peculiar privilege. And now I will grapple with the noble Lord [Palmerston] on the ground which he selected for himself, in the most triumphant portion of his speech, by his reference to those emphatic words, *Civis Romanus sum*. He vaunted, amidst the cheers of his supporters, that under his administration an Englishman should be, throughout the world, what the citizen of Rome had been. What then, Sir, was a Roman citizen? He was the member of a privileged caste; he belonged to a conquering race, to a nation that held all others bound down by the strong arm of power. For him there was to be an exceptional system of law; for him principles were to be asserted, and by him rights were to be enjoyed, that were denied to the rest of the world. Is such, then, the view of the noble Lord, as to the relation that is to subsist between England and other countries? Does he make the claim for us, that we are to be uplifted upon a platform high above the standing-ground of all other nations? . . .
    What, Sir, ought a Foreign Secretary to be? Is he to be like some gallant knight at a tournament of old, . . . challenging all comers for the sake of honour, and having no other duty than to lay as many as possible of his adversaries sprawling in the dust? If such is the idea of a good Foreign Secretary, I, for one, would vote to the noble Lord his present appointment for life. But, Sir, I do not understand the duty of a Secretary for Foreign Affairs to be of such a character. I understand it to be his duty to conciliate peace with dignity. I think it to be the very first of all his duties studiously to observe, and to exalt in

* Lord Macaulay, (1800–1859), the historian and a frequent contributor to the Whig *Edinburgh Review*.

honour among mankind, that great code of principles which is termed the law of nations . . .

Sir, I say the policy of the noble Lord tends to encourage and confirm in us that which is our besetting fault and weakness, both as a nation and as individuals. Let an Englishman travel where he will as a private person, he is found in general to be upright, high-minded, brave, liberal and true; but with all this, foreigners are too often sensible of something that galls them in his presence, and I apprehend it is because he has too great a tendency to self-esteem—too little disposition to regard the feelings, the habits, and the ideas of others. Sir, I find this characteristic too plainly legible in the policy of the noble Lord . . .

No, Sir, let it not be so: let us recognise, and recognise with frankness, the equality of the weak with the strong; the principles of brotherhood among nations, and of sacred independence. When we are asking for the maintenance of rights which belong to our fellow-subjects resident in Greece, let us do as we would be done by . . . Let us refrain from all gratuitous and arbitrary meddling in the internal concerns of other States, even as we should resent the same interference if it were attempted to be practised towards ourselves.

W. E. Gladstone, House of Commons, June 27, 1850 (Hansard, 1850).

1853 Budget

15 I have shown you that if you grant us the taxes which we ask, to the moderate amount of £2,500,000 in the whole, much less than that sum for the present year, you, or the Parliament which may be in existence in 1860, will be in the condition, if it shall so think fit, to part with the income tax . . .

While we have sought to do justice, by the changes we propose in taxation to intelligence and skill, as compared with property—while we have sought to do justice to the great labouring community of England by further extending their relief from indirect taxation, we have not been guided by any desire to put one class against another; . . . and we have the consolation of believing that by the proposals such as these we contribute, as far as in us lies, not only to develop the material resources of the country, but to knit the hearts of the various classes of this great nation yet more closely than heretofore to that Throne and to those institutions under which it is their happiness to live.

W. E. Gladstone, House of Commons, April 18, 1853 (Hansard, 1853).

16 It [the Budget speech] has raised Gladstone to a great political elevation, and, what is of far greater consequence than the measure itself, it has given the country the assurance of a *man* equal to great political necessities, and fit to lead Parties and direct Governments.

Charles Greville, *The Greville Memoirs* (London, 1887).

Dislike of Palmerston

17 There was, as is well known, no cordiality in the relations between Lord Palmerston and Mr. Gladstone. Indeed, it is probable that no two men ever sat together in the same Cabinet for six consecutive years who had less in common with one another, or who understood each other so little . . . Mr. Gladstone used to say, not wholly in jest, that in attending Cabinet meetings in 1859–65, he not unfrequently took the precaution of carrying his resignation 'in his pocket'. It was not that he failed to respect Lord Palmerston's high qualities as a leader of men and a leader in Parliament. But to Mr. Gladstone, Lord Palmerston appeared to be too ready to sacrifice interests at home to interests abroad; and while excellent at 'sounding the big drum', to be commonly credited with a larger amount of political courage than that to which he was properly entitled.

Sir Edward W. Hamilton, *Mr. Gladstone* (John Murray, 1898).*

The Irish Question

18 In 1868, proposals for dealing with Church and Land Questions in one Act of Parliament were submitted to Bright,** and in acknowledgment he wrote the following remarkable letter to a friend in Ireland:

* Sir Edward Walter Hamilton, (1847–1908), private secretary to Gladstone from 1873–1874 and again from 1880–1885. He knew Gladstone, who was a friend of the family, from an early age.
** John Bright, (1811–1889), reformer, M.P. and Minister under Gladstone, who later opposed Gladstone's Home Rule Bill.

TAKING THE (IRISH) BULL BY THE HORNS.

The Mansell Collection

My Dear Sir,— ... For twenty years I have always said that the only way to remedy the evils of Ireland is by legislation on the Church and land. But we are met still with this obstacle, even yet I fear insurmountable, that the legislation must come from and through a Parliament which is not Irish. ... The Whigs are almost as much afraid as the Tories are of questions affecting the Church and the land, and they seem to have almost no courage.

Lord Russell is old, and cannot grapple with a great question like this. Mr. Gladstone hesitates, and hardly knows how far to go ... I suspect he has not studied the Land Question, and knows little about it. ... The Liberal Party is not in a good position for undertaking any great measure of statesmanship. Some Whigs distrust Mr. Gladstone, and some, who call themselves Radicals, dislike him. He does not feel himself very secure as leader of a powerful and compact force. The Whig peers are generally feeble and timid, and shrink from anything out of the usual course. We want a

strong man with a strong brain and convictions for a work of this kind, and I do not see him among our public men . . .
I am, very sincerely yours,
JOHN BRIGHT
R. Barry O'Brien, *John Bright* (Thomas Nelson & Sons, n.d.).*

Disraeli's Attack

19 As time passed it was not difficult to perceive that extravagance was being substituted for energy by the Government. The unnatural stimulus was subsiding. The paroxysms ended in prostration. Some took refuge in melancholy, and their eminent chief** alternated between a menace and a sigh. As I sat opposite the Treasury Bench the Ministers reminded me of one of those marine landscapes not very unusual on the coasts of South America. You behold a range of exhausted volcanoes. Not a flame flickers on a single pallid crest. But the situation is still dangerous. There are occasional earthquakes, and ever and anon the dark rumbling of the sea.
Speech by Benjamin Disraeli at the Free Trade Hall, Manchester, April 3, 1872 (London, n.d.).

Resigns Leadership

20 The following letters have been forwarded to us for publication:—
11, Carlton-house-terrace, S.W., Jan. 13.
My dear Granville,—The time has, I think, arrived when I ought to revert to the subject of the letter which I addressed to you on the 12th March.
    Before determining whether I should offer to assume a charge which might extend over a length of time, I have reviewed, with all the care in my power, a number of considerations both public and private, of which a portion, and these not by any means insignificant, were not in existence at the date of that letter.
    The result has been that I see no public advantage in my continuing to act as the leader of the Liberal Party; and that,

*Richard Barry O'Brien, (1847–1918), barrister and author of many books including a life of Parnell.
**i.e. Gladstone.

at the age of sixty-five, and after forty-two years of a laborious public life, I think myself entitled to retire on the present opportunity. This retirement is dictated to me by my personal views as to the best method of spending the closing years of my life.

I need hardly say that my conduct in Parliament will continue to be governed by the principles on which I have heretofore acted; and, whatever arrangements may be made for the treatment of general business and for the advantage or convenience of the Liberal Party, they will have my cordial support. . . .

Believe me always sincerely yours,
W. E. GLADSTONE.

Carlton-house-terrace, Jan. 14.

My dear Gladstone,—I have received your letter of the 13th.

I have communicated to you in detail the reasons which make me profoundly regret and deprecate the conclusion at which you have arrived.

Your late colleagues share these feelings to the fullest extent, and have regretted the failure of their endeavour to persuade you to come to a different decision.

We have no doubt that the liberal Party, in and out of Parliament, will feel as we do on the subject. . . .

Yours sincerely,
GRANVILLE*

The Times, January 15, 1875.

Gladstone on the Bulgarian Horrors

21 By a slow and difficult process . . . but not through our own Parliament, or Administration, or establishments abroad, we now know in detail that there have been perpetrated, under the immediate authority of a Government to which all the time we have been giving the strongest moral, and for part of the time even material support, crimes and outrages, so vast in scale as to exceed all modern example, and so unutterably vile as well as fierce in character, that it passes the power of heart to con-

---

* Lord Granville, (1815–1891), Foreign Secretary under Gladstone from 1870–1874, who became leader of the Liberal party in the Lord's on Gladstone's resignation of the leadership.

ceive, and of tongue and pen adequately to describe them. These are the Bulgarian horrors; and the question is, What can and should be done, either to punish, or to brand, or to prevent? . . .

Let me endeavour very briefly to sketch, in the rudest outline, what the Turkish race was and what it is . . . They were, upon the whole, from the black day when they first entered Europe, the one great anti-human specimen of humanity. Wherever they went, a broad line of blood marked the track behind them; and, as far as their dominion reached, civilisation disappeared from view. They represented everywhere government by force, as opposed to government by law. . . .

Twenty years ago, France and England determined to try a great experiment in remodelling the administrative system of Turkey, with the hope of curing its intolerable vices, and of making good its not less intolerable deficiencies . . . The successes of the Crimean War, purchased . . . by a vast expenditure of French and English life and treasure, gave to Turkey for the first time perhaps in her blood-stained history, twenty years of a repose not disturbed either by her herself or by any foreign Power . . . The insurrections of 1875 . . . have disclosed the total failure of the Porte* to fulfil the engagements which she had contracted under circumstances peculiarly binding on interest, on honour, and on gratitude. Even these miserable insurrections, she had not the ability to put down . . . A lurid glare is thrown over the whole case by the Bulgarian horrors . . .

I entreat my countrymen . . . to require and insist, that our Government, which has been working in one direction, shall work in the other, and shall apply all its vigour to concur with the other states of Europe in obtaining the extinction of the Turkish executive power in Bulgaria. Let the Turks now carry away their abuses in the only possible manner, namely by carrying off themselves. Their Zaptiehs and their Mudirs, their Bimbashis and their Yuzbachis, their Kaimakams and their Pashas,** one and all, bag and baggage, shall, I hope, clear out from the province they have desolated and profaned. This thorough riddance, this most blessed deliverance, is the only reparation we can make to the memory of those heaps on

---

* Porte, or Sublime Porte, the seat of government of the Ottoman, or Turkish, empire in Constantinople.
** Titles given to government employees.

heaps of dead; to the violated purity alike of matron, of maiden, and of child; to the civilisation which has been affronted and shamed; to the laws of God or, if you like, of Allah; to the moral sense of mankind at large. There is not a criminal in an European gaol, there is not a cannibal in the South Sea Islands, whose indignation would not arise and overboil at the recital of that which has been done, which has too late been examined, but which remains unavenged; which has left behind all the foul and all the fierce passions that produced it, and which may again spring up, in another murderous harvest, from the soil soaked and reeking with blood, and in the air tainted with every imaginable deed of crime and shame.

W. E. Gladstone, *The Bulgarian Horrors and the Question of the East* (London, 1876).

A Turkish View of Gladstone

22 A Turkish newspaper . . . printed a detailed biography of 'the man Gladstone, projector of mischief.' This set forth how he was 'born in 1796, the offspring of the headlong passion of a Bulgarian named Demitri, the servant of a pig merchant named Nestory.' He went to London in charge of some pigs his master desired to sell. Desiring to pass himself off as an Englishman, he changed his Bulgarian name, Grozadin, to Gladstone. 'His gluttony for gold makes Gladstone look yellow. According to those who know him he is of middling height with a yellow face, wearing closely cut whiskers in the European style, and as a sign of his satanic spirit his forehead and upper forehead are bare. His evil temper has made his hair fall off, so that from a distance he might be taken for quite bald.'

Henry W. Lucy, *The Right Honourable W. E. Gladstone* W. H. Allen & Co., 1895).

English Attacks

23 Here is the bitter, hurtful, and if I permitted myself your keenness of language I might add, the repugnant side to your appeal on behalf of outraged humanity. Your pamphlet is one word against the Turk, and twenty against the Tory. It is long since I experienced a keen party emotion; but I have not yet

ceased to be an Englishman, and I therefore feel that when men who have served their country with fidelity and distinction, be they Tories or Liberals, are weighted with the cares of office, it is a crime against patriotism for the humblest or the most exalted individual to hamper their hands and embarrass their action, in an anxious and disquieting crisis arising out of foreign complications, by what in ordinary times might pass as the tactics of party, but at such a moment can only be stigmatised as the arts of faction. For if your pamphlet be not one long, acrimonious indictment against the Ministry, what then is it? . . .

I have the responsibility neither of office nor of an elevated position; but I speak with that sense of responsibility which every man must feel in formulating a tremendous accusation, when I most solemnly declare that I believe the blood of every murdered Bulgarian peasant, the dishonour of every violated Bulgarian mother and maid, the mangled limbs of every mutilated Bulgarian child, to lie at the door of Russian diplomacy and Russian ambition. The punishment of the Bulgarians may have been out of all proportion to the provocation they gave, but it was Russia that incited, fomented, and fed the Bulgarian disturbances. It was Russia that allowed Prince Milan of Servia to declare war against Turkey, and urged the mountaineers of Montenegro to the same infelicitous enterprise. It is Russia which is now watching how far peace or war will best serve her purposes; and Russian diplomatists, I will pledge myself, are at this moment chuckling with laughter, which you would probably think fiendish could you hear it, over the credulous sentimentality of your inopportune pamphlet.

Alfred Austin, *Tory Horrors, or the The Question of the Hour* (London, 1876).*

Midlothian Campaign

24   It was on November 24 [1879] that Mr. Gladstone soon after eight in the morning quitted Liverpool for Edinburgh, accompanied by his wife and Miss Gladstone. 'The journey from Liverpool,' he enters, 'was really more like a triumphal procession.' Nothing like it had ever been seen before in England.

---

* Alfred Austin, (1835–1913), a journalist and minor poet who was appointed Poet Laureate by Lord Salisbury in 1896.

Statesmen had enjoyed great popular receptions before, and there had been plenty of cheering and bell-ringing and torch-light in individual places before. On this journey of a bleak winter day, it seemed as if the whole countryside were up. The stations where the train stopped were crowded, thousands flocked from neighbouring towns and villages to main centres on the line of route, and even at wayside spots hundreds assembled, merely to catch a glimpse of the express as it dashed through. At Carlisle they presented addresses, and the traveller made his first speech, declaring that never before in the eleven elections in which he had taken part, were the interests of the country so deeply at stake . . . When he reached Edinburgh . . . the night had fallen upon the most picturesque street in all our island, but its whole length was crowded as it has never been crowded before or since by a dense multitude, transported with delight that their hero was at last among them . . .

All that followed in a week of meetings and speeches was to match. People came from the Hebrides to hear Mr. Gladstone speak. Where there were six thousand seats, the applications were forty or fifty thousand. The weather was bitter and the hills were covered with snow, but this made no difference in cavalcades, processions, and the rest of the out-door demonstrations.

John Morley, *The Life of William Ewart Gladstone* (Macmillan, 1903).

Apologies to Austria

25 The first thing Mr. Gladstone did on coming into office was to make a contemptible apology to the Emperor of Austria. The London *Times* of May 12th, 1880, said his letter was 'probably without a precedent in the annals of modern diplomacy'.
Mr. Gladstone, Edinburgh, March 17th, 1880. 'What has the policy of Austria been . . . Austria has been the steady, un-flinching foe of freedom in every country of Europe. Austria trampled Italy underfoot; Austria resisted the unity of Germany; Austria did all she could to prevent the creation of Belgium; Austria never lifted a finger for the regeneration and constitution of Greece. There is not an instance, there is not a spot upon the whole map where you can lay your finger and say, "There Austria did good".'

Mr. Gladstone, to Count Karolyi, May 4th, 1880—'At the moment when I accepted from the Queen the duty of forming an administration, I forthwith resolved that I would not, as a Minister, either repeat, or even defend in argument, polemical language in regard to more than one foreign power which I had used individually when in a position of greater freedom and less responsibility . . . I at once express my serious concern that I should have been led to use terms of censure which I can now wholly banish from my mind.'
J. H. Bottomley, *The Conservative's Brief against the Gladstone Administration* ('England' office, the Strand, London, 1884).

The Gladstone Menu

26 A Grand Banquet (or General Mess) at the Boers Head Hotel immediately after the Sale of the Effects of Mr. John Bull carefully prepared by Mr. W. E. Gladstone.

Soups
Peace Soup   White Liver Soup
Entrees
Irish Stew with Buckshot Sauce   Toady in the Hole
Savouries
Hashed Turkey with Mulled Porte
W(h)ines and other Beverages

The Banqueting Room will be appropriately decorated for the occasion with White Feathers.
The Gladstone Menu (London, 1881).*

Second Ministry criticised

27 Lord Palmerston left a legacy of a Liberal majority of 120. In the General Election of 1868 this was fully sustained; but a few short months of office, and the current of popular feeling cooled, to be accentuated at the closing of Mr. Gladstone's six years' administration by a considerable falling off in his majority, and a distinct intimation on the part of the constituencies at all bye elections that his popularity had seriously

* Extracts from a broadsheet issued after the Gladstone government had given self-government to the Boers in the Transvaal following their defeat of the British at Majuba in the first Boer War in 1881.

"WAIT TILL THE CLOUDS ROLL BY!"

suffered. Mr. Disraeli, in two sentences, on the eve of the election of 1874, summed up the case against Mr. Gladstone by the statement 'that he had harassed every interest in the country, and had seriously lowered our influence abroad.'. . . For six years of arduous government, carried on in the face of a most unscrupulous opposition, the Ministry under Mr. Disraeli, afterwards Lord Beaconsfield, . . . thoroughly satisfied the country . . . The invective and misrepresentations of Midlothian had their effect; and as will be well remembered by Mr. Gladstone's followers, the memorable election of 1880 yielded a Liberal majority of 120. Since then, the reversal of his predecessor's foreign policy has landed Mr. Gladstone in serious difficulties in Egypt, Africa and Afghanistan; his Irish policy has culminated in the most coercive of measures, trade is shrinking all round, and society is torn by a multitude of vexatious questions, well calculated to estrange classes, to promote disunion, and directly tending to the disintegration of the national unity and the national Empire. A sustained stream of resignations of prominent officials has testified to the divergence of opinion in the Liberal camp itself upon every important subject, and the bye elections have demonstrated, without a break almost, the decided change that has passed over the English constituencies, in their opinion of the performance of the Liberal Ministry.

H. Crickmay, *A Reply to Midlothian* (Effingham Wilson, London 1884).

Second Midlothian Campaign

28 The fate of the campaign was clear before Mr. Gladstone had got half-way through his first address. It was not to be a repetition of 1880. Its admirers, who affirm that it was a 'triumphant success' may be perfectly right as regards the streets and the railway stations. Those who retort that it was a 'blank disappointment', come nearer the truth as regards the the speeches themselves.

In its outward pageantry the three days' campaign was a brilliant success, without doubt. No impartial witness will deny that, the more so as it has very little to do with the ultimate issue.

As a street lion Mr. Gladstone has no rival, and as showmen our Liberal Committees in Scotland are equally beyond competition. In the spectacular part of its business the Scottish Caucus has improved on its Birmingham model*. . . .

To use an American phrase . . . the Liberal 'machine' in Scotland is perfect, and all its power was exerted to make a brilliant success of Mr. Gladstone's visit. There were only about two thousand electors to accommodate at each of the Corn Exchange meetings. The organising Committee had therefore at their free disposal nearly three thousand seats on each occasion. They very shrewdly distributed these among the Liberal Committees, not in the neighbourhood merely, but all over the country. Each Committee had a certain number assigned to it in proportion to its membership, and they had to be paid for at the rate of half-a-crown per head. Provincial delegates came in by hundreds, and there was perhaps not a town of any note south of Inverness unrepresented at one or other of the meetings. In each case less than half of the audience consisted of *bona fide* electors. The rest Mr. Gladstone might have branded as 'foreigners' had they been caught at any other demonstration than his own. All the audiences were consequently in the fullest sympathy with him. They had been skilfully selected and marshalled with that view. Every requisite condition of an oratorical triumph had been prepared beforehand, and so carefully prepared by men who thoroughly knew their business that visible failure was well nigh impossible.

An Eye-Witness, *The Anti-Climax in Mid-Lothian*, A Review of Mr. Gladstone's Campaign in 1884 (William Blackwood & Sons, Edinburgh, 1884).

29 To thousands of his countrymen Mr. Gladstone has for some years past been far more than a political leader. Even hero-worship does not adequately express their slavish attitude of mind towards him. He has been to them a divinity who feels for them, thinks for them, speaks for them, acts for them . . . He has been their prophet, their saint, their Mahdi.** The grandest of imposters, however, has but his day, and Mr. Gladstone's is evidently drawing towards its moral as well as its physical sunset.

Mr. Gladstone is no doubt gifted with special qualifications

*The efficient party organisation introduced by Joseph Chamberlain in Birmingham in 1878, which was copied by Liberals in other parts of the country.
** The Moslem Messiah.

for the peculiar position he holds as a political demi-god. In his hands clap-trap had been raised to a gospel, and statesmanship has been degraded into trickery of the tongue. He is absurdly out of place in a community making any pretence to the power of intelligent self-control . . . Over an order of civilisation which demands reasoning and a cultivated sense of justice, he casts the glamour of a subtle eloquence more appropriate to a twelfth-century crusade than to a nineteenth-century Legislature. The spell he practises is a witchery of words and phrases rather than of ideas . . . The moment he exchanges the mantle of the preacher for that of the statesman, our Mahdi is 'found out'. He is as powerless and fatuous in administration as he is domineering in debate.

'The Mahdi of Midlothian', *Blackwoods Magazine*, September, 1884.

Gladstone on Home Rule

30 I do not know how many gentlemen who hear me have read the valuable work of Professor Dicey* on the Law of the Constitution. No work that I have ever read brings out in a more distinct and emphatic manner the peculiarity of the British Constitution in one point to which, perhaps, we seldom have occasion to refer—namely the absolute supremacy of Parliament. We have a Parliament to the powers of which there are no limits whatever, except such as human nature in a Divinely-ordained condition of things imposes. . . .

It is commonly said in England and Scotland—and in the main it is, I think, truly said—that we have for a great number of years been struggling to pass good laws for Ireland. We have sacrificed our time; we have neglected our own business; we have advanced our money—which I do not think at all a great favour conferred on her—and all this in the endeavour to give Ireland good laws. That is quite true in regard to the general course of legislation since 1829.** But many of those laws have been passed under influences which can hardly be described otherwise than as influences of fear. Some of our laws have been passed in a spirit of grudging and of jealousy . . . Our first effort at land legislation was delayed until so late a period as the year 1870 . . .

* Prof. A. V. Dicey, (1835–1922), lawyer, writer and Fellow of All Souls (see following extract).
** The year when the Catholic Emancipation Bill was passed.

I do not deny the general good intentions of Parliament on a variety of great and conspicuous occasions, and its desire to pass good laws for Ireland. But let me say that, in order to work out the purposes of Government, there is something more in this world occasionally required than even the passing of good laws. It is sometimes requisite not only that good laws should be passed, but also that they should be passed by the proper persons. . . .

The principle that I am laying down I am not laying down exceptionally for Ireland. It is the very principle upon which, within my recollection, to the immense advantage of the country, we have not only altered, but revolutionised our method of governing the Colonies. I had the honour to hold office in the Colonial Department . . . fifty-one years ago. At that time the Colonies were governed from Downing Street . . . England tried to pass good laws for the Colonies at that period; but the Colonies said— 'We do not want your good laws; we want our own.' We admitted the reasonableness of that principle . . . We have to consider whether it is applicable to the case of Ireland. Do not let us disguise this from ourselves. We stand face to face with what is termed Irish nationality. Irish nationality vents itself in the demand for local autonomy, or separate and complete self-government in Irish, not in Imperial, affairs. Is this an evil in itself? Is it a thing that we should view with horror or apprehension? . . . Sir, I hold that it is not.

W. E. Gladstone, House of Commons, April 8, 1886 (Hansard, 1886).

Dicey's Case against Home Rule

31 The Constitution will cause disappointment and inconvenience both to England and to Ireland.

Englishmen will on the Gladstonian Constitution coming into operation find to their great disappointment that they have not attained the object which from an English point of view was the principal inducement to grant Home Rule to the Irish people, that is, freedom from the difficulty of governing Ireland . . . Home Rule is not Separation, and nothing short of Irish independence would greatly lessen English responsibility . . . The army in Ireland—and no one supposes that England can withdraw her soldiers from the country—will be the British Army under the control of the British Government . . . Hence it follows that the British Ministry remains at bottom responsible for the maintenance of peace and order throughout Ireland. Note the results. If there are riots at Belfast; if unpopular officials are assassinated in Dublin; if evictions give rise to murder in Kerry, the British Army must in the last resort be called in to restore peace or punish crime . . .

That the Gladstonian Constitution cannot satisfy Ireland is all but certain . . . It cannot . . . by any possibility remove the admitted causes of Irish discontent. It cannot tempt capital towards Ireland, but it may easily drive capital away from her shores; it cannot diminish poverty; it cannot in its direct effect assuage religious bigotry; it cannot of itself remove agrarian discontent . . .

A. V. Dicey, *England's Case against Home Rule* (John Murray, 1886).

'Perverted Politics'

32 In relation to Ireland, he [Gladstone] has proved an evil-doer and a false prophet throughout . . . Mr. Gladstone's hands are already virtually reddened with the blood of heroes. But this blood, of which he seems so regardless, and which in point of *quality* leaves nothing to be desired, is small in *quantity* compared with what would flow if he had his way. The predicted amity between England and Ireland is pure moonshine. Give her Mr. Gladstone's Home Rule, and disloyal Ireland will hit befooled England with redoubled strength and bitterness. She will work for complete separation, and will win it . . . The hatred that has been nursed so long, and which has been only intensified by untimely concession, will not be dissipated because Mr. Gladstone, in his old age, has chosen on the spur of the moment, to turn politically heels over head. The hate is durable, and will, alas! endure beyond the day of Mr. Gladstone. On the other hand, an empire still manned by Britons . . . will not die without a fight.

It is with a feeling of moral nausea that I read reference after reference to 'our venerable leader'. Would that I could discern either in his work or in his character any basis for veneration! He is a calamity to Britain, and through her, to the cause of ordered freedom throughout the world. Is he not responsible for the seditious unrest in Ireland which followed his speech on the disestablishment of the Irish church?* . . . Is he not responsible for legislation in Ireland which has falsified his promises, and proved a course of unmitigated disaster? . . .

The Home Rulers in the House of Commons number 277, eighty-six of whom are Parnellites.** The British contingent, therefore, numbers 191. Unionist Britain outweighs Disruptionist Britain in the ratio of two to one. . . . I have spoken of the British Separatists as a handful . . . Not one of these gentlemen was ever heard to utter a syllable sympathetic with Home Rule—they were, on the contrary, its virulent and vituperative foes—until, one fine morning, Mr. Gladstone changed his creed, and published his 'bull' enunciating the new doctrines . . .

What has caused this sudden and astounding change in our idolised politician? What has converted him, to all intents and purposes, into a traitor to his country and a misleader of his friends? Mainly, of course, the unsteadiness of his own character, which makes him the sport of circumstance.

John Tyndall, *Perverted Politics* (William Blackwood, 1887).***

Chamberlain breaks with Gladstone

33 It was something to have the principle of full justice to Ireland solemnly enunciated in the House of Commons by the foremost of English statesmen. Mr. Gladstone's act was fateful, and the historical assembly that listened to his speech did not outmatch the grandeur of the occasion. But the painful scene between him and Mr. Chamberlain**** revealed a state of things that every true Liberal must deplore. It was evident that the 'grand old man' theory had been pushed too far; that Mr. Gladstone had concocted his Home Rule scheme without proper consultation with his colleagues; and that Mr.

* In 1869 the first Gladstone ministry passed an Act disestablishing the Irish Church from January 1, 1871, so that the Irish no longer had to support a Protestant Church to which most of them did not belong. The Act aroused intense opposition among Protestants in Ireland and England.

** Charles Stewart Parnell, (1846–1891), leader of the Irish party in the House of Commons. His political career ended in 1890 after he had been cited in a divorce case.

*** John Tyndall, (1820–1893), the physicist, born in Co. Carlow, Ireland, who was elected F.R.S. in 1852.

**** Joseph Chamberlain, (1836–1914), leader of the radical wing of the Liberal party, whose opposition to Home Rule split the party.

Chamberlain, in particular, had been treated very cavalierly . . . Mr. Chamberlain had rendered signal service to the Liberal party, and Mr. Gladstone had no right to treat him as a pedagogue treats a schoolboy, or a chieftain a retainer . . . He deserved consideration, therefore, when Mr. Gladstone was devising how to meet the claims of Ireland, as the un-acknowledged, yet real leader of the advanced Radicals.

Mr. Gladstone, however, thought, or at least acted, other-wise. Mr. Chamberlain was treated as a mere subordinate officer, whose only business was to take his general's orders when they were ready. Those who now denounce Mr. Chamberlain's 'vicious ambition' must have very slavish souls themselves to imagine that a man of his standing should have tamely suffered such abasement. They might also reflect that political morality cannot gain by their treating every man as a renegade who will not submit to dictation, but insists on thinking for himself. Some of them appear to fancy that Mr. Gladstone is the only person in England with a conscience, and the idea that Mr. Chamberlain is animated by conviction in opposing Mr. Gladstone's measures never crosses their minds . . .

Whether his views be right or wrong, he has shown a fine example of independence and resolution, which is much needed in these days of party despotism. Nor are we sure that his views *are* wrong. On the contrary, we think they are mainly right. Nay, we go farther, and maintain that he has shown the instinct of a statesman in fixing upon certain features of Mr. Gladstone's measures as vital errors. Mr. Gladstone, for instance, deliberately proposed to exclude the Irish members from Westminster; since then, however, he has wavered; and now he almost hints that their exclusion or retention is indifferent. Mr. Chamberlain, on the other hand, has all along seen this to be a vital matter, coloring, nay governing, the whole future relations between England and Ireland.

G. W. Foote, *Gladstone's Irish Stew* (London, 1886).*

Wait Till the Clouds Roll by, Billy

34   Billy, our grand old Champion,
            Long Life and health to thee,

---

* George William Foote, a free-thinker, who wrote many pamphlets including a number which were critical of Gladstone.

Long may the Peoples' William
The Peoples' Leader be!
What though some may now desert thee,
Yet victory for us is surely nigh,
Then Billy our grand old champion
Wait till the clouds roll by.

Chorus
Wait till the clouds roll by, Billy,
Wait till the clouds roll by,
Billy our Grand old champion,
Wait till the clouds roll by.

The Shamrock, Rose and Thistle,
The three entwined in one,
This shall be our union,
And not of sword and gun.
Then stand to your post like men undaunted
Home Rule shall be our battle cry,
Billy again our Premier,
If we wait till the clouds roll by.

Wait Till the Clouds Roll by, Billy (London, 1887).

Not a Radical

35 In the eyes of some people, he was a conspirator against the
Constitution, determined to undermine its pillars—'the unscrupulous and destructive demagogue,' the advocate of dis-
ruption, especially in connection with his Irish policy. This
belief had in reality no foundation . . . The fact is, Mr.
Gladstone's mind was essentially constructive, not destructive
—conservative, not radical . . . He was an absolute slave to
precedent and tradition, to recognised forms and established
procedure. He had no disposition towards, much less love for,
change for the sake of change, and he would only recommend change when he had convinced himself that it was
calculated to assist in maintaining the institutions of the
country. Those institutions he regarded not only with respect,
but with affection and pride. He looked upon them much as
the owner of a fine ancestral hall looks upon his possession . . .

He tolerated, and indeed, often advocated, change, because
he regarded it as a lesser evil than persistence in a course

which was known to be wrong; but there was no 'radicalism' in the ordinary acceptation of the term, in his nature. He was a great moderating and controlling force. Extreme people would listen to him when they would hear no one else. He was the ballast in the political ship.

Sir Edward W. Hamilton, *Mr. Gladstone* (John Murray, 1898).

LATER ASSESSMENTS

Morley's Praise

36 Then his passion for economy, his ceaseless war against public profusion, his insistence upon rigorous keeping of the national accounts—in this great department of affairs, he led and did not follow. In no sphere of activities was he more strenuous, and in no sphere, as he must well have known, was he less likely to win popularity . . .

In a survey of Mr. Gladstone's performances, some would place this of which I have last spoken, as foremost among his services to the country. Others would call him greatest in the associated service of a skilful handling and adjustment of the burden of taxation; or the strengthening of the foundations of national prosperity and well-being by his reformation of the tariff. Yet others again choose to remember him for his share in guiding the successive extensions of popular power, and simplifying and purifying electoral machinery. Irishmen at least, and others so far as they are able to comprehend the history and vile wrongs and sharp needs of Ireland, will have no doubt what rank in legislation they will assign to the establishment of religious equality and agrarian justice in that portion of the realm . . .

He was one of the three statesmen in the House of Commons of his own generation who had the gift of large and spacious conception of the place and power of England in the world, and of the policies by which she could maintain it. Cobden and Disraeli were the other two . . . But Mr. Gladstone's performances in the sphere of active government were beyond comparison.

John Morley, *The Life of William Ewart Gladstone* (Macmillan, 1903).

'A Man of Peace'

37 It must be admitted that there were some important Departments of State in whose affairs he never took any interest; in fact, I think it might be said that the only two in whose business he was naturally and genuinely interested were the Treasury and the Board of Trade. As Prime Minister he was, of course, obliged to think about foreign affairs, and he saw all the Foreign Office drafts and despatches; but this to him was generally task-work, and, except in cases when his generous and laudable interest in the 'oppressed nationalities', in Turkey or elsewhere, took effect, his criticisms and suggestions were few, and nearly always in the direction of peace, non-intervention, and *laisser-faire*. I was for the last fifteen years of his life Under-Secretary of State for India; during that time I saw him very often and he talked very freely to me, but I doubt whether he ever spoke to me about Indian affairs. I never heard him say a word which showed the slightest interest in the Navy or the Army, except in so far as their cost, which he was always anxious to cut down, affected the Estimates . . . If ever there was a statesman who deserved to be called 'a man of peace', Mr. Gladstone was that man.

Lord Kilbracken, *Reminiscences* (Macmillan, 1931).*

Few serious errors

38 Recent critics are fond of alleging by assertion and innuendo that Mr. Gladstone's political career was a sequence of errors. All leading statesmen make mistakes, sometimes many in a short time. Mr. Gladstone himself admits that he was no exception to the rule. But successful performance has to be weighed against mistakes. For most detractors a comprehensive allusion to Jefferson Davis,** Majuba,*** Gordon,**** and Home Rule is enough . . .

* Tom Arthur Godley, first Lord Kilbracken, (1847–1932), civil servant, principal private secretary to Gladstone, appointed permanent under-secretary of state for India in 1883.

** Jefferson Davis, (1808–1889), President of the Confederate States of America during the Civil War. Gladstone created a world-wide sensation by supporting him and the secessionist southern states in a speech at Newcastle in October, 1862.

*** Majuba Hill, Natal, South Africa. Scene of a major British defeat in 1881 during the first Boer War.

**** General Gordon, (1833–1885), killed after a long siege of Khartoum in the Sudan. Many people blamed Gladstone for not sending a relief force earlier.

Apart from actions which were and still are matters of political opinion, Mr. Gladstone's serious errors were remarkably few. A leading statesman for forty years, he was in office for nearly thirty. The length of time gave an almost unprecedented opportunity for errors. Yet their totality, relatively to length of time, is small. Weigh the errors against the things achieved in trade and finance, in the Civil Service and legislation, in the promotion of international good-will and peace, in the guidance of new and turbulent forces to loyal acceptance of all that was best in the Constitution, and then let judgment be given.

Viscount Gladstone, *After Thirty Years* (Macmillan, 1928).*

MODERN VIEWS

Leading Liberal in Europe

39 When Gladstone died in 1898 it was universally recognised that he had been the leading figure of the nineteenth century in the history of Liberalism, not only in Great Britain but in Europe . . . Yet for the first twenty-seven years of a career devoted to politics he had been a Conservative . . . When the Conservative party broke up in 1846 he remained loyal to its leader Sir Robert Peel, and was one of the most conspicuous of the band of 'Peelites' who wandered between the two great parties for the next thirteen years . . . He then decided that his agreement with Palmerston's Italian policy and the existing crisis in Italy made it his duty to join the Liberal Government which Palmerston was forming, and he remained in it until its Prime Minister died in 1865. From that time Gladstone was a Liberal leader, for by then he could be nothing less than a leader in any party to which he belonged. Yet it is clear that as a Peelite he looked back wistfully to his old party as a lost Eurydice. 'The key to my position,' he said once, 'was that my opinions went one way, my lingering sympathies the other.'

Once a Liberal, Gladstone differed from all other Liberal leaders both in the tone of his politics and in the source of his principles. Yet his moral ascendancy over the party that he led

---

* Herbert John Gladstone, (1854–1930), M.P. and first viscount: youngest son of his more famous father.

was almost unrivalled. He was as much the idol of the working classes in the eighties as Palmerston had been, in the fifties, the idol of England represented by the ten-pound householder . . . Though he became leader of the party of reform, Balfour* could write truthfully in 1895 that he 'is, and always was, in everything except essentials, a tremendous old Tory'.

J. L. Hammond and M. R. D. Foot, *Gladstone and Liberalism* (English Universities Press, 1952).

Remained a Peelite

40 It is most misleading to describe Gladstone as a 'radical' in any but a most carefully qualified sense. He never became a democrat, certainly never an egalitarian. His democratic sympathies had a moral origin . . He had very little knowledge of the 'social problem' as a whole or in any aspect—much less than Disraeli, for instance. He had no real awareness of what the masses thought. He never modified his Peelite economic ideas. He had little understanding of and less sympathy with all the tendencies characteristic of the period after 1870. He was moving not from right to left in the conventional manner, but rather into a lofty station of his own, remote from the main political course. . . .

Gladstone's politics had become, in fact, sublimely self-centred. He did not know the masses, or care very much what they wanted. It was simply that on certain questions which Gladstone conceived as turning on a moral issue, and which excited his imagination, he found he could employ mass enthusiasm in a righteous cause . . . Gladstone was an Early Father of the Church embroiled in the questions of the nineteenth century.

R. T. Shannon, *Gladstone and the Bulgarian Agitation,* 1876, (Thomas Nelson & Sons, 1963).

Opposition to Socialism

41 Gladstone always opposed the doctrine of socialism, while remaining most insistent that the poorer classes should be enabled to earn a fair share of the national wealth which they helped to create. He regarded freedom for individual effort

* Arthur James Balfour, (1848–1930), nephew of Lord Salisbury, whom he succeeded as Conservative prime minister in 1902.

as morally superior to state intervention: men and women should rely upon self-help, not the State, to improve their lot, and those who were successful had the duty to assist those who were not.

* * *

Intellectually a dogmatic churchman, he was spiritually a man with an evangelical conscience to which he made himself accountable for his every thought, word, and deed. He regarded every undertaking in life as a vocation. . . .

For him government came to mean self-government, but not in the political sense alone: every one was responsible for government of self, as well as being his brother's keeper. He took this double responsibility upon himself, and uniquely sought to impress it on the world.

E. G. Collieu, *Gladstone* (Oxford University Press, 1968).

Irish Policy

42 Parliament reassembled in January 1893, and in February Gladstone introduced his second home rule bill. Unlike the first, it provided for continued Irish representation at Westminster, but this concession to the principle of parliamentary union between the two countries did nothing to placate the opposition; the bill was fiercely contested at every stage; and only a ruthless application of the closure enabled the government to force it through the commons by September. A week later, it was overwhelmingly rejected by the house of lords. Very reluctantly, Gladstone accepted this defeat; he neither went to the country, nor resigned, but simply allowed the bill to drop . . .

With the failure of the home rule bill Gladstone's political career came to a close; and in March 1894 he resigned the premiership. He was the first major British statesman to consider seriously the implications of the parliamentary union between Great Britain and Ireland, and to realise that if Ireland were indeed an integral part of the United Kingdom, it must be governed on the same principles as the rest; and it was this realisation that prepared him to accept the policy of home rule. His importance in the history of Anglo-Irish relations lies less in the measures that he actually carried, far-reaching though they were, than in the immense influence that his concern for Ireland had on British public opinion. It was he, more than anyone else, who made the state of Ireland an issue in British politics.

J. C. Beckett, *The Making of Modern Ireland, 1603–1923* (Faber and Faber, 1966).

PUNCH, OR THE LONDON CHARIVARI.—JANUARY 30, 1886.

THE LIVE SHELL.
(WHICH OF 'EM WILL THROW IT OVERBOARD?)

The Mansell Collection

5. Marquis of Salisbury, 1830-1903

Was the Marquis of Salisbury a reactionary at home and a 'splendid isolationist' in his attitudes to foreign affairs? Such views of him were extremely common after his death, but many modern historians no longer consider them to be entirely true.

Lord Salisbury was a member of one of the ancient aristocratic families of England—the Cecils of Hatfield House, Hertfordshire (3–4). As a young man Lord Robert Cecil—as he was then known—was ordered to take a long voyage for his health, and in 1851 he went to South Africa and, then, in the following year, to Australia and New Zealand (10). On his return home he was elected Tory M.P. for Stamford in 1853. Throughout his life he was known for the outspoken nature of his views (5–9). In 1865 his elder brother died and he became known by the courtesy title of Lord Cranborne. In the following year he was appointed Secretary of State for India in the Derby government, but in 1867 he resigned because of his opposition to parliamentary reform, of which he had always been a persistent critic (11).*

He succeeded his father as the third Marquis of Salisbury in 1868. Although he had opposed Disraeli over the Second Reform Bill, neither men held a grudge and in 1874 Salisbury agreed to serve under Disraeli in his old post of Secretary of State for India (12). In April, 1878, he was appointed Foreign Secretary and he played a major role at the Congress of Berlin.** On Disraeli's death in 1881, he became leader of the Conservative party.

In June, 1885, Gladstone was defeated on a Budget vote and resigned. Salisbury became prime minister for the first time, but in the ensuing election in December, 1885, he failed to secure a majority (13–14). He became prime minister again

* See also pp. 147–8.
** See pp. 91–2.

in August, 1886, following Gladstone's defeat on the Home Rule issue. Salisbury's second ministry, from 1886 to 1892, was responsible for the Local Government Act of 1888 and the abolition of most fees for elementary education in 1891, but his main concern was with foreign affairs (15). For most of the years while he was prime minister he also acted as foreign secretary. He was prime minister again from 1895 to 1902. In all, he served as prime minister for thirteen years and ten months, a total length of time exceeded in the nineteenth century only by Lord Liverpool.

After his death, there were varying opinions whether he had much understanding of the people he ruled (16–17). In modern times, there has been more sympathy for his domestic policies (18) and an almost total rejection of the idea that his foreign policy was one of 'splendid isolation' (19–21).

Further Reading

A. L. Kennedy, *Salisbury, 1830–1903* (John Murray, 1953).
Lilian Penson, *Foreign Affairs under the third Marquis of Salisbury* (University of London, the Athlone Press, 1962).

CHARACTER AND APPEARANCE

Acrid Temper

1 Lord Robert looks older than thirty-four. His bearded face is not youthful; his head at the top is partially bald; his hair is getting somewhat thin and straggling; he might well pass for forty-four. When Lord Robert came into Parliament the soothsayers of the Carlton prophesied that he would make a figure there and speedily rise to eminence in the State. The prophets, however, have been disappointed; for he had held no office, and has not achieved a lofty position in the House. . . . How is it then, that he, with his high connections, talents, accomplishments, and speaking ability, has not risen to a higher position in the House than that which he occupies? . . . The answer must be that Lord Robert Cecil's pride and uncontrollable temper have kept him down . . . Lord Robert's acrid temper is not explosive; there are no eruptions; it is, if we may say so, a sort of chronic low fever; and, though he seldom offends against the rules of the House so grossly as to call upon the Speaker to interfere,

he never rises but he says something sharp, biting, and offensive.
William White, *The Inner Life of the House of Commons*
(T. Fisher Unwin, 1897).

A majestic Figure

2 But in the House of Lords he was perfectly and strikingly at home. The massive bulk, which had replaced the slimness of his youth, and his splendidly developed forehead made him there, as everywhere, a majestic figure. He neither saw, nor apparently regarded, his audience. He spoke straight up to the Reporters' Gallery, and, through it, to the public. . . . He spoke without notes and apparently without effort. There was no rhetoric, no declamation, no display. As one listened, one seemed to hear the genuine thoughts of a singularly clever and reflective man, who had strong prejudices of his own in favour of religion, authority and property, but was quite unswayed by the prejudices of other people. The general tone of his thought was sombre . . .

But though he might find little enough to praise in a world which had departed so widely from the traditions of his youth, still, this prevailing gloom was lightened, often at very unexpected moments, by flashes of delicious humour, sarcastic but savage. No one excelled him in the art of making an opponent look ridiculous. . . .

He was by nature as shy as he was short-sighted. He shrank from new acquaintances, and did not always detect old friends. His failure to recognise a young politician who sat in his Cabinet, and a zealous clergyman whom he had just made a Bishop, supplied his circle with abundant mirth, which was increased when, at the beginning of the South African War, he was seen deep in military conversation with Lord Blyth, under the impression that he was talking to Lord Roberts.*

But, in spite of these impediments to social facility, he was an admirable host both at Hatfield and in Arlington Street —courteous, dignified, and only anxious to put everyone at their ease.

George W. E. Russell, *Prime Ministers and Some Others*
(T. Fisher Unwin, 1918).

* Earl Roberts, (1832–1914), supreme commander in the second Boer War, 1899–1902.

Hatfield House

3 After we were married* we lived for some time at Hatfield**
and in Arlington Street . . . The Cecils lived at Hatfield as a
family, going away for necessary work, or occasionally for
social duty, but always returning home, and marriage making
very little difference to their way of life. . . . Of course the house
was a big one and we each had our own valets and maids and
those with children had their own nurses and nursery maids. . . .

The family, even if they were dragged away by their professions or duties during the week, were always at home at the
week-ends and we habitually sat down thirteen or fourteen to
dinner . . .

Dinner was always served in the great Marble Hall and
was—in those days—a lengthy affair—six courses at least, and
generally seven, besides dessert. There was a lavish splendour
in the service, the numbers of menservants, the quantity of
food and the abundance of wine and the dessert, with home-
grown grapes all the year round and every fruit in season
massed in great dishes. But the Cecils thought very little about
what they ate or drank and nothing at all about how it was
presented to them. The crockery and linen were of the plainest
and the men's liveries seldom smart. I must make an exception
for Lord Salisbury. He had a very fine palate for wine and I
believe he noticed everything even though he said little about
what went on . . .

I feel sure that if I had suddenly asked him how much
beeswax was used every year at Hatfield—which is panelled
with oak and other unpainted wood from attic to basement—
that he would have known. It must have been tons, though the
oak panelling was also rubbed down every autumn with beer.

Viscountess Milner, *My Picture Gallery, 1886–1901* (John
Murray, 1951).

Scientific interests

4 I know no more interesting study in history,' he [Salisbury]
says, 'then those periods when great forces of this kind first

---

* The writer, Violet Georgina, Viscountess Milner, who died in 1958, married
Lord Edward Cecil, fourth son of Lord Salisbury in 1894. He died in 1918 and three
years later she married Viscount Milner.

** Hatfield House, the family home of the Cecils in Hertfordshire, which was
built by the first Lord Salisbury at the beginning of the seventeenth century.

appeared, when they were beginning the work of which nobody suspected the width or the intensity, and one only saw the first elements of its greatness . . .'

We are living, Lord Salisbury thinks, in one of these periods now, and the force that is destined to effect the coming revolution is electricity. . . .Lord Salisbury has harnessed this mighty force at Hatfield. He has made electricity his hand-maiden. It lights up Hatfield House with the light from two thousand lamps. It works an ice-machine in the basement and the ventilator on the roof. It grinds the corn, pumps the water, and drives all the machines on the farm. It dredges the weeds from the river bed. It pumps the town sewage into a tank at the rate of two thousand gallons an hour . . .

It is a strange paradox—the Tory in the State and the Revolutionist in the workshop.

Arthur Mee, *Lord Salisbury* (Hood, Douglas and Howard, Clifford's Inn, London, 1901).*

CONTEMPORARY VIEWS

Salisbury's Policies

5 Of course we cannot certainly *know* what the lowest classes of England would do if they were placed in power, for we have not tried. The experiment, unfortunately, is a nervous one to make, for if it fails it cannot be retraced. Political power that has descended from a higher class in society to a lower, is never yielded back except to a despot. But a specimen of what their leaders' views on the subject of property are, was given to the world a short time ago. A number of working men in London were suffering from having been thrown out of employ. A demagogue of some note assembled them to propose to them a project of relief; and his proposition was, simple and without any circumlocution, to seize the estates of some of the largest landowners, and to divide them among the sufferers. . . .

As this gentleman is said to enjoy considerable popularity among the classes who would rule us if manhood suffrage were adopted, there is nothing chimerical in saying that a new Reform Bill would place the rights of property in issue. In

* Arthur Mee, (1875–1943), journalist and editor of weekly *Children's Newspaper* from 1919 to 1943.

truth, every indication which comes to the surface shows that the present unequal division of property is regarded with great jealousy by the multitudes who are almost or altogether excluded from a share . . .To give them political supremacy — or even to give them such a preponderance of power as shall enable them, by future Reform bills, to gain the rest—is to give them the means, which they will not fail to use, of satisfying these desires. . . .Industry is the radiating centre of all social well-being; and industry thrives in precise proportion as property is secure. That the fruits of industry should be enjoyed in peace is the main object for which civilisation exists.

Lord Robert Cecil [later Lord Salisbury], 'The Theories of Parliamentary Reform', *Oxford Essays* (London, 1858).

6 Take another question in which I feel a great interest—the housing of the poor in our large towns. I hope that much good may be done in that direction, and that it may be the privilege of the present generation to assuage a vast amount of human misery. But I see symptoms in many quarters of an inclination to turn men aside from the practical question of how to relieve those evils in order to get up a fight between the landowning class and the rest of the country.

There is a peculiar error to my mind which the Radical politician constantly commits in his efforts to ameliorate the condition of the people of this country. He appears to approach every question in order to find out exciting material for hounding on one class against another. I do not believe that this is progress. We have enormous difficulties to encounter; we have a great population; the sources of prosperity are not flowing so abundantly as in the past, and we find that the opportunities of industry are not numerous, and, therefore, the means of keeping the people from great suffering are engaging the minds and thoughts of political men at the present time. It is a great, arduous, and almost super-human task, and it is a task to which we can only prove equal if we pull together and act together in trying to fulfil it. They are no true friends of progress who persuade you that these objects are to be reached by generating quarrels.

Speeches of the Marquis of Salisbury, Reading, October 30, 1883, ed. Henry W. Lucy, (George Routledge, London, 1885).

7 I want to point out to you another matter with respect to the question of raising the wages of the labouring man. (Cheers) I want to point out to you what seems to me the fundamental difference between the Conservative and the Radical proposals at the present time. The Conservative desire is so to manage affairs as to remove all restrictions, so as to give the necessary stimulus to industry, that you shall advance forward to conquer new realms of industry yet uninvaded, that you shall obtain the entry to markets that are now closed to you—(cheers)—that new markets shall be found for you; that, in short, the well-being of the working man shall be obtained by providing him with fresh material for his industry, and giving him the opportunity of finding in the wealth, which that industry shall create, ample satisfaction of all his wants. (Cheers) The Conservative points the working man 'forward', to obtain wealth which is yet uncreated. The Radical . . . on the contrary, turns his eyes backward, does not help him, and does not tell him to create new sources of wealth, but says that the wealth which has been already obtained is badly divided—(a voice: 'Robbery' and hear, hear) —that some have got something, many have got nothing at all, and that the real remedy is to turn back and fight among yourselves for the wealth that has already been obtained. (Cheers)

Now, I do not desire—I am not here speaking for the rich man—(hear, hear)—he will defend himself; and you will find him to be a very hard nut to crack—(hear, hear)—I am not defending him—I am speaking of the benefit of the community, and especially the provision of work and wages for the working man, and I say that the fatal defect of this Radical panacea which asks you to think of ransom and restitution, instead of looking forward to reaping new wealth in new markets, and making the country richer as a whole—(hear, hear)—its fatal defect is that it will prevent the development of industry . . .

There is no work to be done, there is no wealth to be created unless you have first of all capital to help you. (Hear, hear) It may not be a large capital; it may be little, but the amount must be sufficient to feed the man while he is working, and it must be enough to find him tools to work with. Unless the capital can be found you cannot make the industry go forward, and all efforts to do so must be frustrated.

A Speech by the Marquis of Salisbury to the South London Conservative Associations, delivered in the Victoria Hall, Waterloo Road, November 4, 1885 (Simpkin & Marshall, London, n.d.).

8 In View of our Indian empire and the importance to us of the communications with that empire, we cannot allow any Power to have in Egypt an interest, or an influence superior to our own. (Cheers) That I hold to be in the present time an elementary maxim of British policy. (Cheers) But you will ask me, 'Why is it an elementary maxim?' . . . I will ask you to reflect for a moment on the tenure by which your Indian empire is held. Remember that you are a people holding the Indian empire by the proportion, say, of 250,000 to 250,000,000. You hold that empire because your greatness is acknowledged . . . Your empire is beneficent; nobody would maintain that more strongly than I do. (Hear, hear) It is the highest that you can confer on those distracted people; but because it is beneficent in itself it does not follow that they, or that the leading and moving spirits among them, would necessarily acknowledge it to be beneficent, or would recognise that their own interest was concerned in upholding it; and if once your power is weakened, your reputation lowered, your sword blunted, do not for a moment delude yourselves with the belief that any benefits which you have conferred or any benefits which you can promise will lengthen by a single day your empire in that peninsula. (Cheers) Your power, the power which you use for good, which I believe to be one of the highest means of good that Providence ever confided to a nation, must nevertheless for the present, in the presence of those Indian people be the power, the force of the sword. (Cheers) . . .

It is the truest policy, the brightest heroism, the most genuine philanthropy to maintain your credit—your military credit—in the world, so that no one shall be entitled to dispute it, and so prevent that terrible arbitrament of the field of battle which can only issue in so much carnage and misery to all who have to take part in it . . .

Sentiment in itself makes men better citizens—the belief that they belong to a great empire, with great traditions, with great hopes, ornamented by distinguished names and splendid exertions, that belief I think makes every citizen himself work better in his own sphere, and impresses and purifies the national character by which we all exist. (Cheers) But it does more than this. Undoubtedly we should avoid anything like an unnecessary, intermeddling, adventurous policy. (Hear, hear) But your empire, if we mean it to live, must grow, must steadily grow. If it ceases to grow it will begin to decay. (Loud cheers) That empire . . . is the foundation and the necessary condition of that commercial prosperity and of that industrial activity which are the bread of life to millions of our people. (Loud cheers).

Speech of the Marquis of Salisbury at Plymouth, June 4, 1884, to the National Union of Conservative and Constitutional Associations (1884).

9 We have had an anxious period at the Foreign Office, but we have floated into a period of comparative calm, and I do not intend to worry you with matters which are passed by. There is, unfortunately, one matter which has not passed by, and that is the trouble which afflicts the Turkish Empire . . .*

At first there was in this country a certain number of voices —some of them voices of great weight—raised in favour of isolated action by Great Britain. . . .

There is a very happy and salutary belief in the minds of the British public that the British Fleet can go anywhere and do anything. And, within limits, that belief is to be encouraged. But if you desire by force, and against the will of the existing government, to amend the Government and to protect the industry and security of the inhabitants of Turkish provinces, you can only do it by military occupation. A military occupation is a very large undertaking, which requires a very large military force. No fleet in the world can do it. No fleet in the world can get over the mountains of Taurus** to protect the Armenians. (Laughter and 'Hear, hear'.) . . . Therefore, I hail with great satisfaction the indications which are furnished to us now daily that the public opinion of this country, though roused, and justly roused, by the atrocious horrors of which the Turkish Government has been guilty, has yet seen that for every work there is a fitting instrument; and that the fitting instrument for reforming the government of the Turkish

* Nationalist uprisings in the provinces of Armenia were suppressed by the Turkish government with great brutality between 1894 and 1897.
** A range of high mountains in Turkey which cuts Armenia off from the west.

provinces in the interior of Asia Minor is not the army of an island some 2,000 miles off. (Hear, hear.)

But it may be done by others. You will not be surprised, therefore, as I told you last year, that I see no course which this country can wisely take except that of adhering to the European Concert. If the European States are willing to act they have means of action which we do not possess . . . The European Concert means that six Powers act together. When they act together, of course, there is no difficulty. But any one of them has the power of vetoing their action; and so far that, if that veto is sustained, the European Concert cannot exist . . .

It is said that the Powers are acting on selfish principles. I cannot accept that accusation in any degree; or, at all events, if they are acting on selfish principles in refusing to enter upon a course which may end in a European war, they are pursuing a selfishness which is much to be praised and which ought to be imitated by all . . . You have to remember that if the result of your conduct is a war in the east of the Mediterranean it will not hurt you very much. It may affect some of your commercial and political interests, but no part of the territory of the Queen will be affected and no subject of the Queen will be less safe in his industry and his possessions. But if a war is aroused in the east of the Mediterranean, and spreads to the European empires which adjoin the Turkish Empire, vast populations will be threatened in their well-being, vast industries will be arrested, probably great territorial changes will be set on foot, and perhaps the vital existence of nations may be threatened. You cannot expect nations who are in that position to look upon the problems presented to them with the same emotional and philanthropic spirit with which you, in your splendid isolation, are able to examine all the circumstances.

'Lord Salisbury's speech at the Lord Mayor's Banquet, Guildhall,' *The Times*, November 10, 1896.

Visit to Australia

10 At 10 o'clock we set off . . . in a two-horse cart for Bendigo.* Mr. Cockburn is the commissioner who resides there . . . The commissioner's tent is pitched at some distance

* Bendigo, principal goldfield centre in Victoria, Australia, one hundred miles from Melbourne.

from the actual diggings for the greater convenience of obtaining water. There is a waterhole close by bearing the elegant name of Sheepwash Creek, where he draws his water and the diggers wash their gold. . . .

From this camp the commissioner rules a body of 100,000 men; exacts their licence fees, punishes their offences, and guards their gold. For this latter purpose his only coffer is a tin paper box secured by a sixpenny padlock; and his coercive force consists of three policemen, two carbines and a sword. And yet his tent has never been robbed nor his authority resisted . . . There were but two tents . . . One of these tents was given up to us. In it the dinner was served. It was a solid meal, consisting of damper,* mutton, and potatoes —the two latter half cooked in the embers of the camp fire. We ate these provisions in a species of widened pannikin, something between a wash-hand-basin and a soup plate, ingeniously constructed so as to be inconvenient in either capacity. Such a conventionality as a tablecloth was, of course, not to be expected. But I pitied the poor commissioner, who, being deprived of his only pair of knives and forks by his guests, was reduced to the tantalising expedient of carving with his penknife . . .

It is much to the credit of the diggers that the feebleness and meanness of this establishment does not seem to have weakened their respect for constituted authority. Mr. Cockburn told me a story in point which rather struck me. As the drought of this summer increased, the water-hole which he had appropriated was almost the only one which continued to afford a good supply; and numbers of the diggers, cut off from that, were barely able to get enough to drink. As the prospect increased of dying of thirst, they assembled at the commissioner's tent, and in a body begged him to allow them to use his tabooed water-hole. Mr. Cockburn declined; a fellow was insolent; Mr. Cockburn seized him and locked him up. The crowd might easily have taken for themselves what he refused to grant, and have rescued their comrade from the clutches of his three policemen. But instead of that they peaceably retired, and proceeded to draw up a petition. Then Mr. Cockburn thought it both more just and more prudent to give in. He also told me that whenever he goes among them they are always too glad to appeal to him to settle, as arbitrator, any

* unleavened bread.

differences they may have. They distrust each other's arbitration, but have full reliance on that of one above them.

Lord Robert Cecil's Gold Fields Diary, ed. Sir Ernest Scott, (Melbourne University Press, 1935).*

Salisbury attacks Second Reform Bill

11 I have heard it said that this Bill is a Conservative triumph. If it be a Conservative triumph, to have adopted the principles of your most determined adversary . . . the hon. member for Birmingham;** if it be a Conservative triumph to have introduced a Bill guarded with precautions and securities, and to have abandoned every one of those precautions and securities at the bidding of your opponents, then in the whole course of your annals, I will venture to say the Conservative party has won no triumph so signal as this . . .

After all, our theory of government is not that a certain number of Statesmen should place themselves in office and do whatever the House of Commons bids them. Our theory of Government is, that on each side of the House, there should be men supporting definite opinions, and that what they have supported in opposition they should adhere to in office; and that every one should know, from the fact of their being in office, that those particular opinions will be supported. If you reverse that, and declare that, no matter what a man has supported in opposition, the moment he gets into office it shall be open to him to reverse and repudiate it all, you practically destroy the whole basis on which our form of Government rests, and you make the House of Commons a mere scrambling place for office. You practically banish all honourable men from the political arena, and you will find, in the long run, that the time will come when your statesmen will be nothing but political adventurers; and that professions of opinion will be looked upon only as so many political manoeuvres for the purpose of attaining office . . . I desire to protest, in the most earnest language which I am capable of using, against the political morality on which the manoeuvres of this year have been based. If you borrow your political ethics from the

* Lord Robert Cecil became Lord Cranborne on the death of his elder brother in 1865 and Lord Salisbury on the death of his father in 1868.
** John Bright, (1811–1889), whose championship of the cause of parliamentary reform led, eventually, to the passing of the Second Reform Bill in 1867.

ethics of the political adventurer,* you may depend upon it the whole of your representative institutions will crumble beneath your feet.

Lord Cranborne (later Lord Salisbury), House of Commons, July 15, 1867 (Hansard, 1867).

Reconciliation with Disraeli

12 Differences between public men are always apt to be exaggerated by the observer from without. Yet the breach which has been created between Lord Cranborne** and his chief by the events of 1867 might well seem serious, even to experienced politicians. It is likely, indeed, that smaller men would have been permanently estranged. A statesman of a different temperament from that of Mr. Disraeli might have cherished a grudge against the colleague by whose retirement at a critical juncture his position had been seriously endangered, and who afterwards had not hesitated to oppose him again and again by speech and vote on more than one question, which, if carried against him, would have been fatal to his Government. On the other hand, there are men who in Lord Cranborne's position would have bitterly resented the sudden arrest of an official career of high success and still higher promise, by the uninvited duty of resisting a measure which ought never to have been introduced. But the retired Minister was animated by the patriotism that merges private in public considerations; his chief had the politic magnanimity of the thorough man of the world. . . .

Rumour was, of course, busy during the few days immediately succeeding the resignation of the [Liberal] Government [in 1874] with the imaginary difficulties which were being encountered by Mr. Disraeli in the attempt to carry out the Royal commands to form a new Administration. . . . By the afternoon of the day following the summons of Mr. Disraeli to Windsor, he had already filled the principal places in his Cabinet, and it was officially known that Lord Salisbury would return to his old post at the India Office . . .

H. D. Traill, *The Marquis of Salisbury* (London, 1891).***

* i.e. Disraeli. Cf. also Salisbury's earlier attack on Disraeli, pp. 84–5.
**Later Lord Salisbury.
*** Henry Duff Traill, (1842–1900), journalist and editor of the *Observer* from 1889 to 1891.

Salisbury on the Hustings

13 At this period of his career* Lord Salisbury was forced to yield to the democratic spirit so far as to 'go on the stump' and address popular audiences in great towns. It was an uncongenial employment. His myopia** rendered the audience invisible, and no one can talk effectively to hearers whom he does not see. The Tory working men bellowed 'For he's a jolly good fellow'; but he looked singularly unlike that festive character. His voice was clear and penetrating, but there was no popular fibre in his speech. He talked of the things which interested him; but whether or not they interested his hearers he seemed not to care a jot. When he rolled off the platform and into the carriage which was to carry him away, there was a general sense of mutual relief.

George W. E. Russell, *Prime Ministers and Some Others* (T. Fisher Unwin, 1918).

Liberal Criticisms of Salisbury

14 Let us look on his belief or Political Creed, and try to comprehend Cecilism . . .

Now the first, and, indeed, guiding principle of Cecilism, running through all his speeches and writings, is that he is the Defender of Property. Defence of Property, this he says is the chief end of government. . . . What does it mean? . . . Defence of Property, as interpreted in Cecilism, is that same Defence which we have seen before upheld by Tory champions, which would defend Property from all duties; recognising only its rights, not its liabilities. . . .

The second principle of Cecilism seems also adverse to Progress. 'What drag,' asks the noble Lord, 'is strong enough to stop the vehicle upon which we stand from rolling onwards?' Even I, my noble Lord, weak and unsure even in my own conceit, can answer you this question unhesitatingly! None! Not on this Earth dwells a Power able to stay Progress towards Higher Things . . . Indeed, if this desire to be placed upon a Stationary vehicle were not of quite terrible import to us all, we might almost smile at Cecilism and its Tory dog-cart drawn up under a hedge, with horse out and shafts on the

* In the election campaigns of 1885–1886.
** Short-sightedness. (See also extract 2, p. 145.)

ground, quite satisfied that all necessary driving is over and done for, with something akin to amusement. . . .

Thus far Cecilism, I confess, does not please me. We have little to look for from it at home. What, then, is its chief characteristic in dealings Beyond Seas . . . I think it may be fairly answered in five words, 'Midlothianism* has destroyed our Prestige.'. . . This then, this influence founded not on reason, is what Military Toryism will uphold . . . Alas! if it be that we cannot maintain our influence in Foreign Affairs by right conduct and just dealing; if it needs Prestige to keep these; we had better withdraw from the councils and battle-fields of Europe, acknowledging honestly that we are a mere Sham, a Power not supported by Reason . . .

Yes, Cecilism with its anti-Reform agitation, Defence of Property, Fear of Change, and Worship of Prestige, is on trial, a trial by Combat, with Midlothianism still waving aloft its old flag of Peace, Retrenchment, and Reform, towards which its followers look bravely and full of Hope. These are the Ideals towards which each Party aims, and you, you only, Electors of Great Britain, can decide between them.

Teufelsdrockh Junior, *Gladstone Government* (The Leadenhall Press, 1885).

Achievements of Second Ministry

15 There is no denying that for full six years this Government fought its way victoriously through the House of Commons, though confronted by an Opposition of wondrous resourcefulness and persistency . . . and that it carried out a national policy, as exemplified by the Acts for the better enforcement of the law in Ireland, for the improvement of the relations between the Irish landlords and their tenants, for the purchase of land by tenants in Ireland, for the County Government in England and Scotland, for the reform of the Scotch Universities, for the reduction of the interest on the National Debt. Further, its muster-roll of measures in the second rank was long and imposing—such measures as the regulation of mines, assisted or 'free' education in elementary schools, . . . the granting of Allotments for labourers, the creation of Small Holdings for yeomen . . .

Taking the legislation all in all, we may say that it touched

* The foreign policies expounded by Gladstone in his Midlothian campaign.

almost every part of our national life in its many phases—life under ground, in the mines—life above ground, in the factories, in the market-places, in the alleys and courtyards—life on the farms, the fields, the allotment gardens—life in the counting house and the savings banks—life in the barracks and at sea, and in the bush beyond the sea—life everywhere and under all circumstances as lived by British people.

The foreign, colonial and imperial policy was eminently satisfactory to those foreign Powers who could reasonably be conciliated, and thus tended to preserve the peace. . . . It demarcated the British sphere of influence in Eastern Africa in agreement with Germany, and in Western Africa in agreement with France. Thus, while making territorial arrangements on a vast scale, it strengthened existing ties with two European Powers . . .

No understanding between two independent bodies could be closer or more cordial than that which has subsisted between the Conservatives and the Liberal Unionists* during this Parliament. An agreement, beginning in respect to one grave subject, has extended to many other subjects. A spirit of forbearance and concession has prevailed on both sides . . . On the whole we all believe that this operative alliance, under the generic name of Unionist, is a phenomenon of happy augury for the future of British politics, being based upon faith in the imperial capacity of the United Kingdom.

Sir Richard Temple, *Life In Parliament* (John Murray, 1893).**

LATER ASSESSMENTS

Representative of his Class

16 Salisbury represented more effectively than any leader of the last half-century the best qualities of the governing aristocrat. He was patriotic, self-denying, of exceptional industry and ability. Office to him was only an instrument for the promotion of his country's welfare. At any moment without a murmur or complaint he would have laid down the burden of authority.

* Liberals opposed to Home Rule who left the Liberal party in 1886 and joined the Conservative party.

** Sir Richard Temple, (1826–1902), administrator in India; sat as a Conservative M.P. from 1885–1895.

He thought and fought for his order, not to ensure to them privileges or exemptions, but because he believed that their maintenance did supply the best material for sound and reliable government. Although he lived mostly with his peers, there was nothing egotistical or arrogant in his personality; but he did not know or come sufficiently into contact with the influences, movements and aspirations of classes other than his own.

Lord George Hamilton, *Parliamentary Reminiscences and Reflections, 1886–1906* (John Murray, 1922).*

The Common Touch

17 I do not think that his success as a leader was fully achieved in either House of Parliament. Indeed, except on the comparatively rare occasions when the action of the House of Lords became of critical importance his qualities as a parliamentary chief were scarcely brought to the test. His authority over his following in the House of Commons rested fundamentally upon the authority he possessed in the country. It is no paradox to say that the fact of his being a peer induced a reliance on popular support more constant and direct than would have been called for from a House of Commons leader. He was naturally impelled to minimise the importance of House of Commons decisions, to look always beyond them towards those movements of public opinion which must ultimately determine the existence of a House of Commons majority. It was mainly in this larger field of leadership that of deliberate purpose he exerted his energies . . . He had a large comprehension of the feelings and of the prejudices of the people whom he was called upon to govern. It was to a degree innate in him. He was charged with limiting his sympathies exclusively to the land-owning class. That was not true—but it was true that by temper and character he was essentially a squire and therefore one of a class which has always shown itself pre-eminent in the strength of its intuitive national sympathies. The influence which the squires of England have achieved over their compatriots' minds in the past and which in spite of all the adverse forces ranged against them they still to a great degree maintain, is really founded on the fact that

* Lord George Hamilton, (1845–1927), conservative M.P. and statesman.

they are themselves but archetypes of some of the most prevalent English characteristics.

Lady Gwendolen Cecil, *Biographical Studies of the Life and Political Character of Robert, Third Marquis of Salisbury* (Hodder & Stoughton, n.d. printed for private circulation).*

MODERN VIEWS

Grand Old Man

18 Beginning as the *enfant terrible* of the Conservative Party, Salisbury ended as its Grand Old Man . . . Entering Parliament before the Crimean War, he was in office when Edward VII came to the throne. Leader of his party through three victorious General Elections, he left it still strongly entrenched in power. Had he confined himself to diplomacy, his achievements in the Near East and in Africa would rank him high among the most memorable figures who have presided over the Foreign Office. His general record in home affairs, although less notable than what he accomplished abroad, is not one of stagnation. He introduced free education, remarking that, since the state had made education compulsory, it was unfair that the very poor should be asked to find the money. . . .

It would be easy, but inaccurate, to paint him as diehard. He had no fear of the people; he simply maintained that they were the same as everybody else, and that efficiency in government was not to be achieved by the enforcement of doctrinaire equality. . . . The enfranchised and educated masses did not begin to make themselves felt in Parliament until 1906. Thus Salisbury ruled in the twilight of the political day of which he was old enough to have seen the afternoon sun.

A. P. Ryan, 'The Marquis of Salisbury', *History Today* (April, 1951).

'Splendid Isolation'

19 That Britain's conduct of her relations with other powers was formerly, and more especially during the nineteenth century and at the beginning of the twentieth, governed by a principle,

* Lady Gwendolen Cecil, (1860–1945), daughter of Lord Salisbury and author of 'Life of Robert, Marquis of Salisbury', (1830–1892), 4 vols., Hodder and Stoughton, 1921–1932.

policy or attitude, often described as 'traditional' or 'time-honoured', of 'isolation'—even of 'splendid isolation'—has been the view of many historians. . . . It would be interesting to know who was the first historian, as distinct from contemporary observer, to express this view in print. It seems probable that the first historian to put forward what has since become a widely accepted view was William Harbutt Dawson, who in Volume III of the *Cambridge History of British Foreign Policy*, published in 1923, referred to 'the old national attitude of "splendid isolation" ', for which, he claimed, Salisbury had a 'preference'. It is understandable that an opinion expressed in so well known a work of reference should have exerted much influence on subsequent writers.

Christopher Howard, *Splendid Isolation* (Macmillan, 1967).

20 Traditionally the Anglo-Japanese alliance* has been regarded as the great divide in British foreign policy in this period, on the grounds that it marked the turning from 'splendid isolation' to the policy of understandings and limited commitments which became the basis of British policy in the decade before 1914 and created an increasing involvement in Continental politics. . . .

But it is misleading to confuse this alliance with the British position in Europe. The Anglo-Japanese alliance made no appreciable difference here and it certainly did not end British 'isolation' from the Continent . . . Obviously it had repercussions on the British position in Europe: if nothing else it averted any weakening of the British fleets in European waters. But the effect of this was to make a European alliance less necessary. This was why *The Times*, the most vociferous opponent of a German alliance, welcomed that with Japan with open arms: now there was no reason at all to seek support from Berlin. But, unfortunately, both at the time and subsequently, this has been obscured by the jargon of 'splendid isolation', with its inherent assumption that this was an accurate description of Salisbury's policy over the preceding decades. As has recently been shown, 'splendid isolation' was a term invented not by Salisbury but by his opponent, Chamberlain, in 1898, when he airily declared that Britain had pursued a 'policy of strict isolation' since the Crimean War.

* A treaty signed in 1902 under which Britain promised to be neutral in the event of a war between Japan and Russia, but pledged assistance if any other power came to the aid of Russia.

In fact Salisbury's policy never had been isolationist. 'Isolationist' was a term which he disliked and rarely employed.* From 1886 to 1897 he had worked more or less closely with the Triple Alliance . . .**

C. J. Lowe, *The Reluctant Imperialists, British Foreign Policy, 1878–1902* (Routledge and Kegan Paul, 1967).

Achievement in Foreign Policy

21 A more than superficial study of Salisbury's diplomacy disposes of the view that he was an 'isolationist', in the sense of avoiding every form of contact with foreign nations. British interests in the last quarter of the nineteenth century came into conflict with those of other nations all over the world. Consequently no British foreign secretary could adopt a completely isolated position, even had he so desired. . . .

Of all principles of diplomacy, that of good faith in international relations he held to be the most fundamental. This explains his well-known reluctance to assume new commitments and his faithful discharge of those which he did undertake . . . Salisbury was opposed to signing alliances precisely because he was not certain that a British Government at some future date would honour its provisions. He was never tired of repeating this to foreign ambassadors, but they generally did not believe him and suspected him of a subtlety that was alien to his nature.

Another principle important to an understanding of Salisbury's diplomacy was his belief that, in the last resort, the English people and not the Cabinet were the arbiters of foreign policy. He was always conscious, at times painfully so, that this imposed limits on the conduct of diplomacy . . .

Despite rather than because of the efforts of historians, Salisbury's reputation as a great foreign secretary remains legendary . . . Bismarck, for instance, never got the better of him. The partition of Africa was accomplished without war and Britain gained the lion's share. In an age when the great Powers were vigorously pushing their claims, Britain held her own without joining any of the alliance groupings. All this was

* For one of his rare uses of the term, see p. 152.
** A secret treaty of mutual defence guarantees between Germany, Austria-Hungary, and Italy which lasted from 1882 to the First World War.

not accomplished accidentally. Fashoda* and the Congress of Berlin indeed appear as the two great triumphs of his career, though Salisbury himself would have denied it. Successful diplomacy, he would have claimed, avoids alike both war and spectacular success. War was to Salisbury the ultimate misfortune. A diplomatic victory he considered almost as bad since to humiliate a rival now made the task of conciliation more difficult later on. It is in his careful and patient handling of an immense variety of serious international problems that Salisbury's true greatness is to be discovered.

J. A. S. Grenville, *Lord Salisbury and Foreign Policy, The Close of the Nineteenth Century* (The Athlone Press, University of London, 1964).

---

* In 1898 the French occupied Fashoda on the Upper Nile in an attempt to annex part of the Sudan. Salisbury's firm diplomatic resistance caused the French to withdraw and to renounce their claims.

List of Ministries, 1830-1902

1830–1834	Grey	Whig
	(Palmerston, Foreign Secretary)	
1834	Melbourne	Whig
	(Palmerston, Foreign Secretary)	
1834–1835	Peel	Conservative
1835–1841	Melbourne	Whig
	(Palmerston, Foreign Secretary)	
1841–1846	Peel	Conservative
1846–1852	Russell	Whig
	(Palmerston, Foreign Secretary until December, 1851)	
1852	Derby	Conservative
	(Disraeli, Chancellor of the Exchequer)	
1852–1855	Aberdeen	Coalition
	(Gladstone, Chancellor of the Exchequer)	
1855–1858	Palmerston	Whig
	(Gladstone, Chancellor of the Exchequer, for a fortnight)	
1858–1859	Derby	Conservative
	(Disraeli, Chancellor of the Exchequer)	
1859–1865	Palmerston	Whigs and Liberals
	(Gladstone, Chancellor of the Exchequer)	
1865–1866	Russell	Whigs and Liberals
	(Gladstone, Chancellor of the Exchequer)	
1866–1868	Derby	Conservative
	(Disraeli, Chancellor of the Exchequer)	
1868	Disraeli	Conservative
1868–1874	Gladstone	Liberal
1874–1880	Disraeli	Conservative
	(Salisbury, Foreign Secretary from April, 1878)	
1880–1885	Gladstone	Liberal
1885–1886	Salisbury	Conservative
1886	Gladstone	Liberal
1886–1892	Salisbury	Conservative
1892–1894	Gladstone	Liberal
1894–1895	Rosebery	Liberal
1895–1902	Salisbury	Conservative

Acknowledgements

The author gratefully acknowledges the permission to use extracts from the following copyright material.

J. C. Beckett: *The Making of Modern Ireland.* Reprinted by permission of Faber and Faber Ltd.

Robert Blake: *Disraeli.* Reprinted by permission of Eyre & Spottiswoode (Publishers) Ltd.

Galen Broeker: 'Robert Peel and the Peace Preservation Force' from the *Journal of Modern History* (December 1961). Reprinted by permission of the author and the University of Chicago Press.

G. E. Buckle (Editor): *The Letters of Queen Victoria*, 2nd Series (1926). Reprinted by permission of John Murray (Publishers) Ltd.

Lady Gwendolen Cecil: *Biographical Studies of the Life and Political Character of Robert, Third Marquis of Salisbury.* Reprinted by permission of A. P. Watt & Son on behalf of the Estate of Lady Gwendolen Cecil and the Kraus Reprint Co.

Maurice Cowling: *Disraeli, Gladstone and Revolution.* Reprinted by permission of Cambridge University Press.

Richard Deacon: *The Private Life of Mr. Gladstone.* Reprinted by permission of Frederick Muller Ltd.

Norman Gash: 'Peel and the Party System 1830–1850' from *Transactions of the Royal Historical Society,* 5th series, vol. 1 (1951). Reprinted by permission of the author and the Council of the Royal Historical Society.

Norman Gash: *Mr. Secretary Peel: The Life of Sir Robert Peel to 1830.* Reprinted by permission of the Longman Group Ltd.

Viscount Gladstone: *After Thirty Years.* Reprinted by permission of Macmillan London and Basingstoke.

J. A. S. Grenville: *Lord Salisbury and Foreign Policy: The Close of the Nineteenth Century.* Now available in paperback. Reprinted by permission of The Athlone Press.

J. L. Hammond and M. R. D. Foot: *Gladstone and Liberalism.* Reprinted by permission of the English Universities Press Ltd.

Lord Kilbracken: *Reminiscences.* Reprinted by permission of Macmillan London and Basingstoke.

C. J. Lowe: *The Reluctant Imperialists: British Foreign Policy 1878–1902.* Reprinted by permission of Routledge & Kegan Paul Ltd.

Henry W. Lucy: *The Rt. Hon. W. E. Gladstone.* Reprinted by

permission of W. H. Allen & Co. Ltd.
Sir Philip Magnus: *Gladstone*. Reprinted by permission of John Murray (Publishers) Ltd.
Kingsley Martin: *The Triumph of Lord Palmerston*. Reprinted by permission of Hutchinson Publishing Group Ltd.
Viscountess Milner: *My Picture Gallery*. Reprinted by permission of John Murray (Publishers) Ltd.
W. F. Moneypenny and G. E. Buckle: *The Life of Benjamin Disraeli, Earl of Beaconsfield*. Reprinted by permission of John Murray (Publishers) Ltd.
F. C. Montague: *Life of Sir Robert Peel*. Reprinted by permission of W. H. Allen & Co. Ltd.
John Morley: *The Life of William Ewart Gladstone*. Reprinted by permission of Macmillan London and Basingstoke.
George Peel (Editor): *The Private Papers of Sir Robert Peel*. Reprinted by permission of John Murray (Publishers) Ltd.
A. P. Ryan: 'The Marquis of Salisbury', *History Today* (April, 1951). Reprinted by permission of the author.
R. T. Shannon: *Gladstone and the Bulgarian Agitation 1876*. Reprinted by permission of Thomas Nelson & Sons Ltd.
Paul Smith: *Disraelian Conservatism and Social Reform*. Reprinted by permission of Routledge & Kegan Paul Ltd. and the University of Toronto Press.
Donald Southgate: *The Most English Minister*. Reprinted by permission of the Macmillan Company of Canada and Macmillan London and Basingstoke.
A. J. P. Taylor: *The Italian Problem in European Diplomacy, 1847–1849* (1970). Reprinted by permission of Manchester University Press.
George Carslake Thompson: *Public Opinion and Lord Beaconsfield*. Reprinted by permission of Macmillan London and Basingstoke.
David Thomson: *England in the Nineteenth Century*. Copyright David Thomson, 1950. Reprinted by permission of Penguin Books Ltd.
Albert Tucker: 'Disraeli and the natural Aristocracy', *The Canadian Journal of Economics and Political Science* (1962). Reprinted by permission of the author and the Canadian Political Science Association.
The Marquis of Zetland (Editor): *The Letters of Disraeli to Lord Bradford and Lady Chesterfield*. Reprinted by permission of Ernest Benn Ltd.

Index

The page references in bold type refer to quoted extracts